GUWAYU– FOR ALL TIMES

GUWAYU – FOR ALL TIMES

A COLLECTION OF FIRST NATIONS POEMS

Commissioned by

Red Room Poetry

Edited by

Jeanine Leane

Magabala Books

This is a Magabala Book

LEADING PUBLISHER OF ABORIGINAL AND
TORRES STRAIT ISLANDER STORYTELLERS.

CHANGING THE WORLD, ONE STORY AT A TIME.

First published 2020, reprinted 2020, 2021, 2022, 2023
Magabala Books Aboriginal Corporation
1 Bagot Street, Broome, Western Australia
Website: www.magabala.com
Email: sales@magabala.com

Magabala Books receives financial assistance from the Commonwealth Government through the Australia Council, its arts advisory body. The State of Western Australia has made an investment in this project through the Department of Local Government, Sport and Cultural Industries. Magabala Books would like to acknowledge the generous support of the Shire of Broome, Western Australia.

Magabala Books is Australia's only independent Aboriginal and Torres Strait Islander publishing house. Magabala Books acknowledges the Traditional Owners of the Country on which we live and work. We recognise the unbroken connection to traditional lands, waters and cultures. Through what we publish, we honour all our Elders, peoples and stories, past, present and future.

Cover Design Jo Hunt
Cover Artwork Kamsani Bin Salleh
Typeset by Post Pre-press Group
Printed and bound by Griffin Press, South Australia

ISBN (Print) 978-1-925936-54-4
ISBN (ePUB) 978-1-925936-56-8
ISBN (ePDF) 978-1-925936-55-1

A catalogue record for this book is available from the National Library of Australia

Red Room Poetry is located on Gadigal Country of the Eora Nation, where the threads of *Guwayu* were predominantly woven together.

We first acknowledge and respect Gadigal Elders and Custodians past, present and emerging and Elders and Custodians of the many other Countries where these poems have grown and whose continued culture and languages live in these pages. Always was, always will be …

Our deepest thanks to all our poets who have offered their experiences, time and spirit in these pages and for their energy and care across all the projects they have shaped with Red Room Poetry. More than poems, these are conversations, connections with community, understandings and relationships ever evolving.

A very special thanks to Guest Editor Jeanine Leane who has been essential to the weaving and work of *Guwayu*. The level of care and consideration given by Jeanine to each poem and poet included here lives beyond these pages.

We're also grateful for poets like Lionel Fogarty, Ali Cobby Eckermann, Gayle Kennedy, Jeanine Leane and Lorna Munro who helped to pave the way and introduce other First Nations poets and communities to Red Room Poetry.

To all the Red Room Poetry team past and present who have supported the commissioning process for the poets included in *Guwayu* over the past 16 years, and Kirli Saunders, who has encouraged so many new voices through the Poetry in First Languages project.

Gratitude to Magabala Books and Rachel Bin Salleh who believed in the poetic bones of *Guwayu* from the outset and have given this collection a print home.

Many thanks to our First Nations Advisory Council for guiding the ways we work and the paths of learning and unlearning at Red Room Poetry.

CONTENTS

FOREWORD

Hopefulness still blooms
And remains strong
Claps a beat
Breaks
Through layers
Of questions
We ask ourselves in the stillness
Of contemplation
And stay reminded
That beauty still resides here after 228 years
In silence

LORNA MUNRO, FROM 'DREAMING TRACK'
COMMISSIONED BY RED ROOM POETRY 2015

Guwayu—a Wiradjuri word—means *still and yet and for all times*. Guwayu means all times are inseparable; no time is ever over; and all times are unfinished. *Guwayu—For All Times* releases the arrested times of the Country's First Peoples held captive in the colonial calendar, and frees kidnapped memories held hostage to false claims of settlement, nationhood, sovereignty and justice. In all First Nations languages, there is a word for all times. And now there is a time for these words. *Guwayu* breaks the silence Munro's poem speaks of to unleash the beauty of First Nations words that have been and always will be here.

Welcome! You are now entering into the many Aboriginal Countries of the nation's First Peoples. This is not Australia as you know it. This is Blak Australia–uncut and unleashed on the page.

This new and dynamic collection came together through several projects led by Red Room Poetry. Red Room Poetry is a national not-for-profit organisation that creates poetic projects and learning programs in collaboration with a spectrum of poets, schools, communities and partners for positive impact. The mission is to make poetry accessible to all, especially those who face barriers to creative opportunities.

Since 2003, Red Room Poetry has grown to be Australia's leading organisation for the creation and commissioning of poetry. Reflecting the diversity of contemporary Australian voices, Red Room Poetry embraces all styles of poetry, including page, performance, experimental, musical and visual. Poetry is published and promoted across a range of landscapes, languages and mediums, such as radio, installation, stage, digital spaces, murals, poetic pathways and mapping apps. These imaginative projects increase poetic visibility, vibrancy and engagement.

In the English-speaking Commonwealth of invaded and occupied settler colonies, Red Room Poetry is unique in its ongoing commitment to poetry across many different styles and forms that recognises the voices of new, emerging and established poets, and in its continued commitment to the first stories of place. First Nations songs, stories and languages have echoed across the Countries under this nation from time immemorial. Since its instigation, Red Room Poetry has commissioned, published and provided platforms for First Nations poets, artists, students, Elders and communities to celebrate, strengthen and share our culture. Continuing in their commitment to first voices, Red Room Poetry has cultivated this collection of First Nations poetry to celebrate Culture, Community, Land, Language and Identity–all of which are integral, interconnected and inseparable parts of the deep history of this continent more recently called Australia.

This collection is unique in the following ways: first, this poetry comes from the heart and soul of First Nations communities across Australia. It speaks from the many Countries under the geopolitically federated nation. Second, the collection brings together many voices never heard before, and many new poems from across the length and breadth of the continent, alongside those of more established, previously published poets. Third, the editing and consultation process that underpins this ground-breaking collection is a benchmark in First Nations editing and consultation practice with the poets, Red Room Poetry and Magabala Books. Finally, the diversity of First Nations languages represented in this collection is to date unprecedented in Australian Indigenous publishing–yet long overdue.

Several poems appear in both First Language and English with interpretations provided by community Elders and/or Language Custodians of the many First Nations languages that live and breathe among us on the mainland. The use of the term 'interpretation' rather than translation is a conscious choice and one recommended by participating Elders and Custodians. The term speaks more faithfully to the complexity of each of our languages that are unique and refuse direct classification and translation into the coloniser's introduced language of English. For some poets, too, the decision to craft their works in Aboriginal-English rather than Standard Australian English is a conscious and deliberate choice. It is also a testimony to our ability to make the introduced language our own and to make it work for our many communities, and is further evidence of the innovation and resilience of our First Nations peoples post invasion. Such innovations are transforming the English language and Australian literary studies.

The editing process for this collection adhered to cultural protocols devised and implemented by First Nations writers, editors and community members for Red Room Poetry. As a result, the voices in this collection are largely uncut and uncensored. It is a collection written for and by First Nations from the many communities that form the modern nation of Australia. Much Aboriginal writing in Australia is still subject to imported, introduced and sometimes invasive northern hemisphere, western literary practices. This collection knows no such limits, borders or boundaries. The works within are not trimmed or manipulated or edited by settler editors with a settler audience in mind. This collection is a radical intervention in Aboriginal publishing for its breadth of representation, diversity of language, and drafting and editing protocols.

The collection is organised around the themes of several Red Room Poetry projects: *Extinction Elegies*, *New Shoots*, *Poetic Moments*, *Poetry Object*, *The Disappearing*, *Rhyming the Dead*, *Unlocked* and *Poetry in First Languages*. These projects and the poems realised go beyond the acknowledgement of poetry as an art form to recognising its capacity and far-reaching and lasting impact for social justice, greater community awareness and emotional well-being.

Extinction Elegies creates and records new elegies that reflect on losses and endangerment of Australian species. As countless species disappear due to global environmental change, Extinction Elegies takes the elegy, a poetic form traditionally used to reflect on human losses, and refocuses it through attention to non-human species and their habitats. New Shoots celebrates and cultivates poems inspired by plants and place that deepen cultural connections with nature. Poetic Moments focuses on cultural place-making, creating opportunities for poets to engage, respond and reflect on connections between the temporal and physical landscape. Poetry Object invites poets to create poems inspired by treasured, curious or talismanic objects. The Disappearing uses geolocations to map poetry to place through the charting of fragmentary her/histories, impressions and memories, encouraging readers to interact with the works in a non-linear way. Rhyming the Dead sees poets create new poems inspired by a deceased poet of their choosing. Poems in the Unlocked suite have grown out of a collaboration with poets, students and educational staff from New South Wales correctional centres. This program unlocks the potential of inmates through the reflective and healing power of poetry. Poetry in First Languages, developed by Gunai poet and children's author Kirli Saunders, celebrates, shares and preserves knowledge of First Nations languages and culture through poetry. This project supports First Nations poets, Elders and Language Custodians to connect and to create poetry in First Languages on Country. Poems in this suite feature interpretations in Dharawal, Gundungurra, Gumea Dharawal, Arrernte, Ngunnawal, Barkindji, Gadigal, Yugembeh, Wiiradjuri, Djapu and Pintupi-Luritja. In addition to these projects, the Red Room Poetry Fellowship has seen two fellowships thus far awarded to First Nations poets. Poems produced from these fellowships are also featured in this book.

This extensive collection of First Nations voices is by no means exhaustive. It brings together First Nations poets who have worked on Red Room Poetry projects–there are many more, talented and prolific First Nations poets than those represented here. Many are published in other collections and anthologies–many are still waiting to be heard. And, while

Guwayu is the first collection of First Nations poetry to do many things, it is our great hope that it will not be the last.

Aboriginal Peoples have woven here since time immemorial. Different fibres and materials are used in different regions. Women and men both wove and crafted nets for fishing and hunting and baskets for carrying and gathering. Children were taught to weave as part of a communal process and continuing cultural practice. Baskets and nets are significant vessels for Aboriginal Peoples all across the continent. Each vessel is crafted and woven in a certain way depending on its intended purpose. Some baskets are woven so tightly that they can hold water; others are more loosely woven so as to allow air flow. Nets can be large or small; some have large gaps in the weave to allow some things to pass through while other things are held. Just as weaving is a series of intricately connected threads that loop, twine, coil, spiral and braid, the poets in *Guwayu* loop, twine, coil and spiral words together as threads in a vessel. Like weaving, the spaces between the threads are just as important to the balance and cohesion of each vessel as the fibres of the threads. The poets in this collection weave their carefully chosen words while at the same time leaving spaces for silence and contemplation of First Nations her/histories, present and futures. Just as a basket or net's purpose determines the materials, the content, the type of weave and the shape, so too are the purposes of each poem intimately related to its materials, contents, weave and shape.

Baskets are designed to gather, to hold, to keep things together and to keep contents safe. Nets are designed to be cast wide and deep, to be spread, to hold, to draw in and to give forth their contents. Baskets and nets are essential to Aboriginal food production, yet their purposes are not strictly utilitarian. They are not just material objects–they are carriers, holders, keepers and transporters of important contents, and each vessel is also a holder and carrier of stories of its raw materials, of its makers and of its history in the hands of its makers and its inheritors.

This collection extends the ancient and continuing cultural practice of weaving to words. In *Guwayu*, the page becomes the vessel–the crafted object that carries culture. The making and crafting of each vessel embeds the maker(s) into its final shape and form–its body. The poems in this collection are baskets and nets of the page. Together they are an exquisite vessel of twenty-first century, living Aboriginal culture.

Vessels handed down from one generation to the next. They are worn by the touch of hands and imbued with stories and memories. Entwined within each thread is something of the maker that is retained as baskets and nets are passed on.

The striking geometrical cover image evokes both a weave and a wave. The criss-crossing of lines are the warp and weft of our songs, stories and memories over our Countries. The ripple that swirls across the length of the page is the wave that moves us together as the Country's First Peoples, and connects us with past, present and future in one continuous, unbroken line of movement.

The historical subject of much of the poetry has been carved in the dispossession of the last 232 years, but it speaks to the future of the First Peoples of the First Countries of the nation. These poems refuse the colonial voyeuristic obsession with tragedy and trauma as the ultimate and only contribution of Aboriginal writing to Australian literary studies. Instead, these poems shout and scream all the while insisting that Aboriginal poetry is innovative, astute and transformative literary intervention that extends beyond the boundaries of despair, nostalgia, romanticisation or lamentation for a 'prehistoric, ahistorical past' or a doomed future. The First Nations poetry between these pages rattles, flings, sings and bends the chains and constraints of verse. And it says loud and clear *Guwayu*–we are here for all times.

The Australian literary landscape needs this bold, brave intervention to wake it up from the 232-year slumber and the dream of the settler mythscape. *Guwayu* breaks the silence–feel the beauty–hear our words. Feel the texture of the sublime vessels woven within this living, breathing archive of us crafted from the living literature of our words.

Dr Jeanine Leane

DREAMING TRACK

Lorna Munro

Please disregard the disruptions
Disconnect from the obstructions
The growth of this canopy pleads
Unweave the wires that bind
Recharge yourself and
Re find
Another way to be
See
What was lost but not forgotten all of those years ago
Re align
Your eyes
With what time
Has changed
Be ready to sacrifice
What you see from what you feel
And change your mind
When you see this space
Read
The descriptions that European artists forgot to enclose
Already etched from the soil and ochre
When they spoke of our country with fine paint brush strokes
What is invoked, for you within these mangroves?
Still home to Burran gowa and Girrigan

Just a swamp
Each beach and cove
Outlines of images emerge
Inlets of goannas and snakes
Taking the shape
Recorded by warriors
As they navigated this place
Rebellion thrives within the shadows
Of these trees
As they always will
And always have been
Birds eye view
Seen from the sky
Interpreting creations
As Biamie inscribed them on the lids of many eyes
Inspiring song
Held in memories
Time will tell
Time will tell
What we leave behind
In this wasteland of ideas thought of long ago
Read the seasons
Know the difference and the reasons
The sacredness embodied as we see them
Why are we here?
In this gathering ground

Of ancestors' voices
Rippled
Within the water
Watch
As it ebbs and flows
And remember
To not invade the space
These soldiers of salt
2 ton
Towers piled high out of the wet
Scream don't touch
We once built up wealth
Observe
These estuaries and streams
That have once conceived poison and dreams
Light
Mud stains
On flood plains
Tell how times have changed
In only some ways
Tide
Chases the stars away
Spirit stands strong
While sun rays touch each day
Push the dark away
Push the dark away

And with each day
Learn to read the land in other ways
Hands of the bay
Hold lines describing what was here in the old days
Says a lot more than what the signs say
Find ways
To waste the time away
In the protection of the shade
And hide away
To another time
Where women fished in nowi
And raised warriors strong and in the kindest of ways
These kind of bays
Tell our story
If you find the ways
Follow the inlets and the water
From Pemulwuy's day
The Bay of Cadi to Kamay
Burramatigul to Tubbagulie
To the home of the Dharawal people
And beyond
Hopefulness still blooms
And remains strong
Claps a beat
Breaks
Through layers

Of questions
We ask ourselves in the stillness
Of contemplation
And stay reminded
That beauty still resides here after 228 years
In silence

DRIPPING WITH DECADENCE (BIG HOUSE, BIG WHITE LIES)

Lorna Munro

Big house, big lies, gubbna, white gubbament
Contorted melaleuca
Conveniently furnished with second-hand decadence
Will society ever speak of the secret deals that were made?
In order to showcase marble reminiscent of all the blood that
was laid
Fireplaces speckled with red, yellow and black
A permanent reminder that refuses to fade back
Arched windows, towers, huge ornate door
Makes me sick to my stomach, like my heart just hit the floor
I don't comprehend it, this makes my head sore
When I think about no one seeing beauty in what was here
before
The cliffs, the white sand, beach and the shore
My people gathered here upon the first sunrise for ceremony
and law
Dreams of magnificent ridgelines intercepting highways like
a slow urban crawl
Connected sites of significance, intricate rock carvings,
middens forty feet tall
But these wonders have disappeared, they're not here
anymore

I have retained my identity, of that I am sure
Inheritance; dispossession, pain and poverty
Against the calls of a mixed-race progeny
While you were left to inherit the bounty of the colony
I am discriminated against on an hourly rate
While you and your ignorant spawn continue to spew hate
I live on the breadline, every day is a hustle
While you parade around with your iPhones and tell me to tighten my bustle
You persecuted my people because of religious beliefs
Initiated alien hierarchies, kidnapping puppets, calling them honorary chiefs
Architects of this great nation, nothing but glorified thieves
Terra nullius–no one here so we can do what we please
Genocide, massacre, they all hide behind the wall
Wondering upon stamps of gold in damp dark places, leading to a grand hall
A line-up of history's menacing faces, regal and ready for the jubilee ball
Crystal chandeliers, floral patterns, manicured lawns
Death and destruction devised in the drawing room by appointed pawns
How many lies are locked away, under the vaulted ceiling?
The English called it a 'discovery'
I call it what it is, stealing
Indigenous vegetation and population cleared

Paradise paved with relics to construct your big house
Resistance was feared
Legacy of lies spanning eleven generations
Languages forced to extinction as well as many great nations
Your monument to a foreign power and foreign queen
Built on land that never was yours and never will be
Peaceful settlement an even bigger lie to hide their crimes
How many dead, how many more sacrificed?
How many brave warriors paid the ultimate price?
To build the big house of ghosts on a hill
Still today your white lies kill ...

SPIRIT REMAINS

Lorna Munro

I am as old as time
I am fluid like spoken rhyme
I am still here, even if you refuse to listen to my lesson
I am wise beyond my years, though I wear the clothes of an adolescent
I am confined amongst your 'good will', please spare me your blessing
I am hungry for change although I am weary of the sinister inner essence
I am still here amidst your secret transgressions
I am present
I am unknown
I am that eerie shiver you feel when you're alone
I refuse to leave, this is my home!
I am the gulf, the bay and the cove
I bin 'ere long-time, I have watched this place grow
I continue to transcend beyond the skies, over the seas and deep below
I am a stubborn child, refusing to walk in your shadow
I am the thing in between, hereafter, the very thing you are too afraid to know
I forever sing nature's song, my ode to ole father crow

I inspired the city beats with the sound of my mismatched
  feet, each step thundering an enormous blow
I will remain here even if you choose to go …
I control young minds, load warriors up with the knowledge
  of guerrilla ammo
I counteract your propaganda with my lyrical skills and my
  righteous flow
I am responsible for your paranoia, I am the force that turns
  the most conservative to 'gung-ho'
The very acknowledgement of my existence will force closure
  of your place of business and from your property you will
  have to forgo
I am chaotic
I am still the same
I make sandstone structures shake and quiver at the mention
  of my name
I am enigmatic
Heartfelt, vengeful and a little dramatic
I am forever studied, questions can't be answered from where
  or whence I came
I smile at young women, they praise my face and sing to me
  but never in vain
Wise men talk about me, boys line up to play my game
They are told to beware my disguises and are warned of the
  bringer of pain
I represent the long line of light, an eternal unbroken chain

I had a beloved I adored, you destroyed their spirit in your
attempt to tame
I am condemned to watch on helpless as you assimilate,
torture and continue to maim
I shall remain in spite of the permanent tear-flooded stain
With oppressed thoughts of immense disdain
Recognise my right, you have nothing left to gain
What am I? you ask, who is the cause for such discontent,
what is to blame?
Know that it is I, the law of this land, the creator, the maker
of rain
I am the core, the spirit, the giver of life, and I can take it
back again

HAPPY WAGGA

John 'Muk Muk' Burke

an overview

We're happy–right?
survey says so.
Flowered parks,
roundabouts,
light in the way of
lights.
night life's no longer
Capital,
But............ sports clubs,
pubs–

sports clubs;
RSL
LEST WE FORGET
that place
or places.
All that
fresh blood shed
on far-flung
distant shores:
we've all got more,
for

their loss:
booze galore,
jackpots,
for an electric toss.

medical nemesis

We're happy–right?
doctors wait little-bit long time–
haven't we all?
patient and strong?
now the end's arrived:
unlike some piddly clinic
as in Ngukurr............
Arakoon,
Boree Creek.
Bring the halt–
lame,
weak,
starved and stammered.

Discharged?
Then celebrate
our clubs–
it's all about
YOU.

Illich, spot on!
Wheel in the normal
(admittedly ageing)
and label them
diseased:
ease all manner of
imagined maladies.

afterwards
Funeral parlours?
Yes!
Bone-yards?
Yes!
Crematorium?
Yes!
(understated secularity,
touch of gloom,
piped tunes
sustain
convictions,
balloons confetti-dot
our hot blue shroud.

A wake for those awake?
Yes!
there's clubs,

stately homes,
cake and sherry.

lower and higher learning
Flush with cash?
Not into public trash?
Why not
Privatise the kids?

Charles Sturt University–
a gum-tree uni
poor relation
of
red brick,
Extra-flush with cash?
First in, best dressed
Gr8,
might be worth a bash.

Kindy,
grade,
college,
uni,
got it made
in Wagga.
Blake's dark

satanic
mills
grind out mindless
MBAs, tooth drillers,
and other coffer fillers.

got the travel bug?
visit poor old gran
at the flash facility?
polish up the ute
on Sundays
and Satdy arvos.
Flush with cash?
Calvary?
A raised-up place............
Perhaps it's you?
Perhaps it's me?
Why, for all that lucre
you'd want the blood red sky.

natural beauty
Collins Park,
(a bit on the side?)
botanic gardens,
where sheep and peacocks reside;
and then the Victory Gardens;

iron fountain
playing,
roses of remembrance
swaying,
some semblance of the sacred
flame
framed by granite gates
of late
adorned–
Iraq,
Afghanistan,
soon be
Syria...........
well that's the plan.

feel like praying?
Take your pick.
Grand Saint Mick's,
geriatric
Jesus at Jack's,
Our own hippy Hillsong.

It's all alright,
endless night
one day must cease
our surfeit of pain

must not
increase
in a town like
Wagga–
home of a
quiet uncertain
peace.

BANK OF THE RIVER

John 'Muk Muk' Burke

Commercial Bank
Fitzmaurice Street
Roman arches reminding us..............
transmitting old English
sensibility
concerning solid grace.
Commands respect–a simulacrum of forebears in
another–distant,
unforgotten
half-remembered
place.

Fresh economy,
different setting,
getting rich on
Ancient Ground:
Ancient Ground
extravagant in plenty,
all the good,
a vault of no bounds,
antipodean Aladdin's cave
that freely gave
its all
to all.

You copied Rome–
a pagan pleasure palace
placed on Sacred Ground.

Greed was the creed;
imagined need
financed exotic seed,
a new breed of beast,
elegant streets,
our sacred meeting place of stones
bridged over on a base
of sacred bones.

Mabo and its aftermath
confirmed the permanence
of sturdy Roman banks
and bridges on lagoons
with
turtle,
yam,
sailed overhead
unseeing,
being roads
to sale yards,
golden fields of
wheat,

tobacco,
sugar cane,
beef and mutton.
Will it take
a further
forty thousand years
before you too
disappear?

K1: YELLOMUNDEE

Evelyn Araluen

    Beyond your stage
    the audience murmurs
men and women weep
and silk their skin bare,
for here and gone and taken.
Held by mostly mountains now
you wear crowns
of returning eucalypt:
    I can't see your lashes
    but feel them still soft
like that skin they try to skin
to wear you with words
and all them names they reason
and rub out.

All this might be lonely
unmarked and highwayside
but then the stars come here
to shine the shape of song
and hear you say
    it's nice
    to have someone
    to talk to.

BAHLOO

Evelyn Araluen

For Aunty Gloria Mathews

bahloo
I am watching you watch me
with light carried by voice gentle
            voice soft
voice to call all my world of sound of sight

bahloo
I have turned around the sun
and turned in to you
and left as much of my blood in the soil
as my blood is the soil

in tree hollow
and above the stars
these crowded earths
have pressed against the other
            as they always do
are flown between
in hum in caw in gahr
in spirit shard
            as you teach
in and against me where
I am never as small   as I remember

where I might wake cold
might wake quiet
might carefully make
          the life I don't get
          the home I don't know

or I can choose something else
and be it or not
but always answer the voice
          with always,
          I will be yours
          and carry yours

          sing it back
          slip crescent and wane
          like   fingers in my hair
          like   blood gift to soil
          like you made a star in her
          that mapped me to myself

bahloo
I am only edges at your light
and I thank you for your dew
for your pale face
how you dance upon the river
how you follow me home

THE SMALL CHEST OF SAND

Matthew Heffernan

Aunty with her weathered hands,
smiling face, and fettered candour
reaches out with a gift,
of my manifested mantra.

A small chest, with speckled seeds,
crimson sand, and freckled beads.
Its timeless OMmm, this stagnant seer
constructs my being and disintegrates fear.

A humble vessel, enveloped in scratches,
its sturdy geometry, threaded by latches,
my attachment transcends isolated raptures.
Freedom, from the abattoir, of which I'm a captive.

The crimson sand's fragrance, fluently unassuming,
a little solace from the conspiring and betrayal that is looming,
but from the rain's rage, and sun's kiss,
the unforeseen is blooming.

The genesis of a memory, for moments worth stealing,
this essence that blankets is my psalm while I'm kneeling,
'thank you', the only words for the person it's revealing,
my manifested mantra, I have found my healing.

NGURRPARRINGU (FORGOTTEN)

Matthew Heffernan

Pintupi-Luritja interpretation guided by Lavinia Heffernan

Irriti ngurra Warumpila ngayulu nyinapayi. Pulinguru walpangku ngyunya yunpa pampunu.

A long time ago, I lived on the land of my people, Warumpi.
From the mountains, the wind would blow and caress my face.

Tjinguru irrititja tjilpi tjuta ngayunywanpa ngurrangka nyinangu?
Walpawana tjilpilu warranu tjukurrpa. Waltja tjutatjarra. Walpaya kulinu ... watjilpa wiyangku.

Maybe just like me, a long time ago, the old men sat on that same land of Warumpi. And felt the same wind on their faces, while singing our Tjukurrpa (Dreaming) songs. Surrounded by their families, listening to the wind, and not sad for home and country.

Kunyi! Wiyalpi ngayulu walpa tjamunyatjarra yutitja kulini. Ngurra kutjupangka ngayulu nyinarra ngurrparringu.

Sadly, I don't hear the wind of my grandfathers clearly anymore. I live in a different people's land. I have forgotten.

Kala tjinguru ngayulu tjilpirringkula ngurrakutu yankuku.
Walpa kulitjaku,
tjukurrpa warranytjaku, waltja tjutangku nyakunytjaku,
tjamuku tjukurrpa kulinytjaku. Wiya watjilarritjaku.

But maybe I'll become an old man, and return to the place of my ancestors, to hear the wind, to sing our Tjukurrpa, to be surrounded by families, to hear my grandfathers' Tjukurrpa, and to not be sad for home and country anymore.

YEPERENYE NOTES

Yvette Holt

last night, by the falling waistcoat
                    of a half-caste desert moon
discreetly, deliberately
                    i heel away from somnolent flutes
water-coloured caterpillars and testaments of olde
                    \
into a floral jar of untitled claypans and annotated spinifex
                    inhaling burgundy-stained pages of handwritten
                       riverbeds
silently, incessantly
                    quilling louvred hours of jaundiced memories
                    \
by the rising ceremonial seas of ante merediem
                    echoing curlews ribbon my desiccated tongue
mirroring speech
                    if only occasionally
quite lucidly, most insanely
                    i delight in the sweet palm of darkness

Note

'Yeperenye notes' was written as a poetic cultural observation of the mountainous sleeping caterpillars Yeperenye (Western MacDonnell Ranges), which surround the shell of Mpwernte (Alice Springs). It drips with the chorus of a psychoanalytical poetic approach through ascending language of past and present. The existence of being throughout the ticking of time from sunset to sunrise.

BARKA–MURRDIE (DARLING, BLACK PERSON)

Paul Collis

Barkindji interpretations provided by Kevin Knight and Wayne Knight

Murrdie–Barka
Black person–my darling.

Barka, Barka, murrdie Barkindji murrdie
My darling, my darling, black Barkindji person

Nga, kappa
I will follow.

Nhantarna. Nhantarna ...
Again, again

... *until* makarra thutha palpa
Again, again ... I (will) follow until it rains like ashes

Note

Our waterway–Barka, to us Barkindji people, is so much more than water and fish, much, much more than ebbs and flows, Barka is our spiritual heart. Barka came to us through Dreaming. She is sacred to us. I wrote this poem as my expression of my great love to that waterway, declaring my love and commitment to Barka and Barkindji people and culture forever.

UN-NAMED

Paul Collis

Barkindji interpretations provided by Kevin Knight and Wayne Knight

He strode the bank of the Darling, a stranger.
And claimed it his. (Spit)
The stranger on the bank ...
–that white Jesus, didn't even know her name. (Spit).
Grandfathers' seeing, black eyes wouldna told him–
'Barka. Thas her name. Barka–that one, there. Nhantarna.
Nhantarna. Barka. Barka.'
But the stranger didn't see the smoke of fires Barkindji.
Didn't smell gun powder that lingers on West wind, icy and
old,
the memory of colour.
Instead, he strode the mountains, rum blind–and parked
Lawson.
Wrote white name upon Wiradjuri, in *that* town–where
streets are filled white.
There's ice wind of memory and river voices unheard.
But we won't dance with the fiddle, rummed-up, nor dance
with the Banjo.
Instead, cool fires and smoke, renew our Mother,
and replace the smell of blood and gunpowder
with small feet dancing Wiradjuri dreams in colour.

Note

Henry Lawson, the poet, wrote a famous poem on the banks of the Darling River, 'A Stranger on the Darling'. I'm a Barkindji person, the Darling is no stranger to me ... and I am no stranger to Her.

The Darling River is known to the Barkindji people as 'Barka'–that is Her name. She was made by the beautiful Rainbow Serpent. This poem is announcing that waterway with the Barkindji name of Barka.

Barkindji people love Barka, and we are not strangers to Her.

RAIN DANCING ...

Paul Collis

Barkindji interpretations provided by Kevin Knight and Wayne Knight

Wathu, wiimpatja– wathu Punritj
Make it watharna,
Watharna kumpatja makarra.
Grandfather, Miikika, speak Barkindji to me.
Yaparra yaamari. Yaamari.
Stay Miikika. Paljarta– wait.
Don't leave ngina
Make the sky rumble, rumble
Murrarta, murrarta.
Make the sky rumble, rumble.
Make the sky thultha yaamari

That one–
Barkindji person, clever fulla ...
Make it rain.
Rain, *big* rain– way over there.
Grandfather, clever man, speak to me in Barkindji.
Stay, clever man. Wait.
Don't leave us.
Make the sky rumble, rumble.
Quick, quick ...

Make the sky rumble, rumble.
Make the sky pour here.

Note

Barkindji people know that waterway which white people named Darling River.

We call that waterway Barka. Barka was made by the Giant Rainbow Serpent. Barka is Woman's Dreaming, and the Giant Serpent is a woman's fertility spirit. The Giant Serpent sleeps below the river. Barka is sacred to us Barkindji. I wrote this poem after visiting my hometown of Bourke, seeing Barka struggling, with hardly any water, our great Love, our spiritual heart, is struggling without water. We Barkindji people are spiritually attached to Barka. So, I called a rain dancing from Barkindji spirits to make rain fall and fill our beautiful Barka.

(I AM) A LINE IN THE SAND

Ali Cobby Eckermann

sand
pulse
footprint
track
dance
dune
walk
bone
skin
grass
alive
sand
sit
burrow
imprint
soul

THE EXTINCTION OF KINDNESS (TITLE POEM)

Ali Cobby Eckermann

get out of here someone yells
before the paddy wagons cruise past
a threat of death on rubber tyres

behind garbage bins we gather
hysterical at this insane game
smashing bottles over our heads

in the restaurant you tip your glass
savour food that you did not grow
pay with money you do not merit

once all people sat and ate together
every person sated in understanding
a mutual love the cultural lore

paddy wagons patrol their threats
behind the bins we are starving
we watch kindness become extinct

THE ABYSS OF AN APOLOGY IN AUSTRALIA

Ali Cobby Eckermann

attracted to the neon light of an auction house
they stand in single file, the natives
selling their artefacts for food

one woman weeps clutching a coolamon
etched with kangaroos and sturt desert pea
her grandmother carved from a red river gum

a girl pulls gemstones from her pockets
fossilised birds of ruby red garnets
containing the songs of the old

a young man holds a bundle of spears
crafted by his grandfather before the missionaries
taught him the economy of rifles

a boy offers a branch from the bough shelter
under which his mothers were born
when his family was housed in happiness

another offers a stringless guitar
his uncle had used to write the music
for an award-winning song

an old man with long grey beard
grips music boomerangs in each hand
knowing their silence will be forever

there is little reparation for food
there is no apology for the past
there is no apology for the past

IT'S JUST SO WRONG!

Ali Cobby Eckermann

it's wrong to kill an eagle the old man said
sitting in the dark staring up at the sky
the embers of the campfire away with the wind

that badness gets stuck inside wrong ways
and I thought about that statement for a while
about how self-justification can be a crime

about how every farm is a fiefdom
about how every paddock diverts the natural
about how the need for capital can vile a moral mind

that badness gets stuck inside wrong ways
and we see it now in the newspapers
and we feel it now in the absence in the sky

it's wrong to kill an eagle the old man said
staring up at the sky through his tears
orbs of spirit shining where eagles once flew

we sit outside the courthouse to sing our songs
we sing for the justice that is unjustifiable
we cry when the verdict is given

we sit outside the jailhouse to sing our songs
we sing for the massacres that litter our lands
we sit crying with feathers in our hair

Note
A New Zealand man has been jailed for 14 days and fined $2,500 for poisoning 406 wedge-tailed eagles at three remote properties in Victoria's east in Australia. It's the first time in Victorian history a person has been jailed for wildlife destruction. The farm worker said he poisoned the birds under the direction of his employer. Farm worker Murray James Silvester, 59, pleaded guilty to killing the protected birds at Tubbut in east Gippsland between October 2016 and April 2018. The court was told the maximum penalty for killing so many eagles was more than $350,000, or six months jail.

2560

Ethan Bell

Dharawal interpretations provided by Jodi Edwards

Mingang Budjari– What Good
been a long time since I nandhi– Seen– you in the
  neighbourhood
Still kicking at the same spots

the cycle remains the same
djardjar**bulalwala**– brothers– light pipes
in reverse of needles to the vein.

out of the pan
who's to Blame
forever chained in this society

Gunji know nganung Njindigang– who you– by names,
grudges like rust
holding on to gabar– government/ white-colonial rivalries

The Bangawan yuwinj– old men
are down Dharagang-dha– near to the river
raking up for a sip

crows' feet stamp
weary miilali
passing round the final nip

pour out the honours for the Bangawan midhang– old one–
   Nganung Nangga– who sleep
pour-out the honors for Nirang Budbud– young hearts,
the reckless and strong

we won't gali– dance– to the drum of their beat
we gali, to clapstick and song

MY BEAUTIFUL LAND

Lola McKickett

This interpretation is a part of Lola's journey of learning

Ngany gwabalitj boodja

Ngany djinang baal meeyal djinang-ak
Windjool gwabalitj-ap
Djet-ak, marlak, boorn-ak
Bandang winin nyiny-boorong
Barna, Minga baalabiny-djil
Wort-koorl-al kooraa, nidja, booraawan idjiny.
Kooraa nyiny boodja yidjow noyitj.
Ngany meeyal minditj-boort djinang
Mandjoo wer dakaniny
Naatj yoowart maaloop, baalap wara
Yenkalang noyitj winin
Noyitj, walang-boort
Nidja korambar yenkalang
Ngany koordak boodja gwabalitj

My beautiful land

I open my eyes but do not see
The beauty all around me,
Of the flowers, shrubs and trees
And all life, living there,
Nature as it was meant to be,
Fading with time and prosperity,
From living lands to dead concrete
My eyes are blurred with hazy smog
Tears flowing with destruction and extinction
What is so wrong? It's foreign
Society so bent on,
extinguishing, suffocating, killing
This ever-changing place
My beloved land of beauty

BIGGER THAN SCHOOL STUFF—AUTHOR'S NOTE

I'm still not 100% sure if this is the proper way to publish this. It is not really a poem. It is a piece of oral history. And right now it is incomplete. It continues to evolve. It is a story; and part of its proper telling requires that it is spoken. By me.

I first told this story at Mparntwe (or 'Alice Springs') in 2018. I told it sitting beneath a very old and sacred tree in what is known as the Todd Mall. This particular tree is a significant one for Arrernte people in Alice Springs. It has special significance for the dreaming stories of uninitiated Arrernte men. I am an uninitiated Arrernte man. A number of years ago there was a big new building built very close to this tree: a new piece of infrastructure for the Northern Territory Supreme Court. Around that time, the old tree began to grow sick. I told this story in 2018 during a walking tour held by my Aunty Alison Furber. There are two Alison Furbers: Alison who lives in town (Alice Springs) and has a small cultural walking tour business; and my Aunty Ali Furber, a language-holder and translator whose first language is Central Arrernte and who lives at Mpweringka, about 50 kilometres north of Mparntwe at Burt Creek, our homeland station.

What has been translated here, I managed to do sitting with my Aunty Ali Furber and her husband Michael Gorey out at Burt Creek during winter 2019. We had a great time and I am very appreciative of their time and energy.

I really want to fully translate this story into Central Arrernte myself. And I want to do it on my homelands with my family as part of learning Arrernte properly myself. That will be the proper publication of the work–a reading of a full bilingual translation. After that, I may feel more comfortable committing it to paper. What appears here should be understood as one version of the work; a glimpse into the process of language revival.

I am an Arrernte man from Mparntwe (or 'Alice Springs') but I don't always live there. I grew up there and I am closely connected to my Arrernte family, but as a child I lived largely with my mum in a non-Aboriginal home. When I'm back at Mparntwe it can be tricky to get the logistics and timing right with family, especially family who live out bush. Lots of things can get in the way of spending proper time. Some of those things are personal, some financial, some structural, and sometimes it feels like there are spiritual or metaphysical barriers that get in the way of reconnecting deeply and learning language and culture. Sometimes I feel ashamed that I don't know more, that I don't 'do more'. I suspect that a lot of blackfellas who live between worlds like me feel this way sometimes. It's lonely and it can be hard to talk about. I get better at these recovery processes all the time, but it's not all glory and wondrous reconnection. It's painful and sad, and the truth is that we've lost so much. The culture I grew up in doesn't really value or understand this kind of work.

But people are working to change that. I see a lot of that work, especially this year–the International Year of Indigenous Languages. That's why I've decided that it's important to publish a version of this piece as it is right now–to show that the journey is tricky and doesn't always go according to plan. I am pretty sure the spellings of some of these Central Arrernte words are wrong; and the translation needs editing with my Aunty Ali Furber and perhaps others, but it feels like a good start.

Please take care in reading this and understand that it is an incomplete and evolving oral history; a work in progress, one that takes time and patience.

Declan Furber Gillick

BIGGER THAN SCHOOL STUFF

Declan Furber Gillick

Everyone's sitting on the carpet
except Latoiya, who's sitting under a desk
holding her hair over her face

Ampe mape arle-le aneme Latoiya anyinte
aneme desk-le akwene ingerre artelemele artele

The other bush kids sit in groups,
whispering in Pitjantjatjara, Warlpiri and Arrernte

Ampe arrpene bush-arenye mape
apurtarremele aneme
ankerrireme Pitjantjatjarra, Walpiri ante Arrernte

The town kids are spread out
amongst the few white kids

Ampe town-arenye mapeakgnarkerreme-le
anerrirreme

Tyrone's a town kid
sitting next to me

Tyrone town-arenye
atenge itwele aneme

I help Mr Graham run the maths games
Then I hand out spelling sheets

The help-irleke kaltyele antene antene
Mr Graham maths game-ke
The spelling-pipe anteme

Then I work with Tyrone.

**Kele ayenge Tyrone-nenge
warrekirreme**

When I work with Tyrone,
he's sussing me out

**Ayenge Tyrone-nenge
warrekirreme re
atyenge aparreme**

Tyrone speaks English:
ay, what's your name again?

**Tyrone angalate angeme
'iwene
arritnye ngkwene?'**

Declan what?

'Declan iwene?'

And where you from?

'Anthenhe-arenye unte?'

Here? What? Alice Springs?

**'Nhenhe-arenye? Iwenhe?
Mparntwe arenye?'**

Ay, me too!

'Ah! Ayenge too!'

He holds up his hand and
I slap it high five
We are the same colour

**Re irltye akerne-irreke
Irltye-krene irltye-itye
artweke
Irlhene nyente-terre**

Do you know my brother Daniel?

Yeah bruss, I used to teach him at Bradshaw, I say

Tyrone's eyes grow wide
I can tell that with my baggy jeans and cap,
I'm about the coolest person he knows

After lunch the kids line up
Still the bush kids huddle together

Latoiya, who was sitting under the desk,
wheels around the corner with her head back and
chest out, grinning and screaming with laughter

She calls out in a shrill cackle,
to a couple of bush kids,
in their native tongue

Tyrone's head whips around
He seizes the moment like a dagger
I watch their eyes meet
There's this recognition, a flicker, a crackling
stillness

For a moment, anything could happen

Tyrone smirks and hurls a mouthful of gibberish at
Latoiya
crudely mimicking the subtle tones and undulations
of Arrernte
fashioning them into a torpedo of abuse that ploughs
into her chest

Her torso deflates, her brow darkens
and her shoulders fall forwards
Her face disappears back behind her hair
and she glares out at Tyrone
with the righteous fury of a woman scorned
She snarls under her breath:
two words she knows he'll understand

Fuck you

Tyrone's not hurt
But he's outraged

Oi! Declan! Did you hear her?
Latoiya said 'F.You' to me!

Yeah, I heard, Tyrone, I heard

As Latoiya and the others go inside
I tell Tyrone to sit with me on the low bench
By the racks of school bags

Tyrone, do you know what language Latoiya was speaking?

He shakes his head

She was speaking Arrernte
And do you know whose language that is?

Yeah, that's my language

Yep, I say, *and that's my language too*

That's our language
How you think Latoiya's gonna feel
next time she wants to speak our language at school?

He shrugs
Maybe bad? he says
Yeah, I say, *yeah, maybe she'll feel bad*
She might feel shame
Cos what you did there,
You made her feel shame for that language
For our language

You understand that?

Tyrone, all our families used to speak
that language here
And then slowly people stopped
They lost it.
It got taken away or they forgot it
or it got covered up by that shame
We're lucky we still go it
But if we make people shame for speaking that language,
they're not gonna speak it
And then we won't have it anymore
And our mob will get really lonely for that language
Like lots of us already are
And this country, our country that we're on here,
It gets really lonely for that language too
Do you understand?

Tyrone nods

Bruss, you not in trouble. Not like school trouble
This is bigger than school stuff
You got … we got responsibilities here
We gotta look after that language. Best we can. Ok?

Ok, he says

We walk back into the classroom
And sit down on the mat

ARMS OF A FRIEND

Carissa Lee

For Monterey Cypress

Origin: Mexico, South America

How many hearts have broken beneath your arms?
How often have you wished that you could hold them?
Does it feel wasteful having so many limbs
and not being able to do as others do?
But rather stand stoic, as is expected,
only to house, hold and endure.
How many times have you wished to pick up forgotten
things?
Wished to fly, like the winged friends who come visit.
Perhaps a lovely stretch or rest would be well earned by this
stage,
for it's only natural that forever reaching could make one
grow weary.
Perhaps instead of dreaming of lands from before,
you long for flight, or reaching unreachable things.
With age, height and absolute majesty, you have grown to love
the world moving as periphery, while you aim for sky.
Do you find relief in being a constant, while others flit, slow
and depart?
You are the closest to immortality,
and yet our disposable lives hold such power.

Are you angry when we dispose of things like they are us,
do you smile at our petty loves and injuries,
do you love us as we love you?

GROOVE

Bruce Pascoe

At some point
he must have lifted his head,
looked back at the axe
in his hand,
felt the edge
turned to the horizon where trees dipped to the sea
and he must have said,
it is useless
it is over.
The heart is just a dumb muscle
electricity in the nerve says pump
and it pumps
reliable as a Rollinson and Tippett
steady, dumb, resolute.
We say it feels because we're looking
for the centre
something that is not the mind
or the hand.
Not the hand holding the axe head
forgotten in the groove
not the eye registering
the declension of land to sea
not the mind
with its need to explain

to deny, to resist,
but the centre that brims
with the blood of hope
or can deflate, collapse
at certain knowledge,
knowledge the brain with its sophistry
must resist.
At some point that poisonous vapour
of thought must have breathed on his brain
stung it, cringing in the skull
withering the vibrant essence of a man
the pulsing brain, soured, corrupt and green
recoiling from the hot breath of gas
like the retracting horns of crushed snails,
a gas that collapses the balloon
we call the heart
and, that man, drawing his hand away from the stone
would have pressed it to his chest
because the pain there was exquisite
complete,
it is over, it is gone.
Not one life, not one thought,
not the groove in the rock,
because it's still there today,
but a whole world,
entire thought

the complete map of the known world;
why stars shine
why darkness exists between them
why a baby is born
how to turn those babies into men and women
how to fathom existence
how to revere its perpetuity,
the obligation to ensure its protection.
That's the gas
that stole into his brain
poisoned the balloon's air.
I have not protected,
I have not ensured perpetuity,
I have failed,
me,
after all the methodical success
of galaxies of generation
stretching across time so vast
rock slabs are laid down as stone
mountains appear where none were before
deserts invade oceans
animals become opals,
across that time, all were successful,
it is me, just me, it is I who have failed.
One tiny phial of that gas
and the city is dead

the city of the mind
of the spirit
of the soul
the essence of life that springs
a curled head of tight green from the soil,
that directs fish to follow the glass wall of waves
that is there behind the mild gaze of kangaroos,
all that,
all that and the gas steals upon it
and corrupts.
The yam pasture is forgotten
the wicker gate to the fish trap
is ajar
drifting back and forth with each tide
mindless in its obedience to the moon
no hand to slip the peg
that secures the gate
to hold the fish
so neatly, so economically
so necessarily, just a useless woven mat
drifting back and forth
like the thoughts of a man
who has lost his mind,
no-one to slip the peg of reason.
The forest creeps and we are not there
to wring our hands at the waste,

no-one to till the garden
keep the forest at bay with flame since the time when Towerer
gave us fire from his tail.
This is just scrub now, no garden,
no copse of trees on the plain
just for their artifice, for their glory,
a tangle of scrub, we now call bush
and lay in front of bulldozers to protect.
Even the memory of fire
has been lost,
the memory of the garden, where trees five hundred years old
are allowed to grow
for the birds,
for the animals, for the fruit,
for the simple grace of their beauty.
Gas, creeping gas,
you think we just laid down and died?
It was the gas of doubt,
the gas of certainty,
it is gone, it is over.
Alright, alright, you say,
are you done now,
have you said it all,
have you told us of our guilt,
your loss,
are you done,

is it over?
So we are guilty
are you happy?
Does our guilt bring back
the stone to the hand
the fire to the land
the peg to the gate?
No, but does your regret
recall the gas from the chamber,
restore the hope,
rekindle desire,
draw the fish along the glass wall of the wave?
And what have you done with the fish?
But here we are on the rocks
above the falls
and our Reeboks
assemble by the grooves,
our caps dip their peaks
like sad birds
to inspect the handiwork of great grandfathers
great grandmothers.
It is so close, you see,
only several generations
since the hands that may have
slipped the peg,
lit the brands,

tilled the land
fell useless by their sides.
The feet here,
shod in latex and nylon,
the caps stitched with the names
of American baseball teams
are removed only a hundred years
from the hands and feet of the grinders,
the peg slippers,
the tillers,
the firers whose bodies must
still be here, close enough for us
to feel the yearning of their spirits.
Is it all gone,
is it over,
if these feet
are back beside the groove
fingers sliding on grandma's polished stone?
Is it over?
Who said never?
Who said no way?
Who said we will overcome some day?
Will we do it with nicotine addiction,
a delusion of grog,
chuckling at the buffoonery
of TV champions?

Will we do it
by begging money
from those whose guilt we prime with a wicked pump?
Will we do it by painting up
and dancing for the governor,
the queen,
the mayor who is wondering
if we're really human at all?
How will we do it,
my brothers,
my sisters,
my aunts,
my uncles,
my mother?
Shall we paint a flag,
raise a tent,
write a song,
kick a ball?
How do you recall gas from the air?
My heart is with the man
holding the stone
stilled in the groove
a second before his heart
releases gas,
because I'll never know what he knew
never even know the profundity

of pain in his stupid muscle
we call the heart
even though I've spent my life imagining that moment.
All that is left is the groove
in the stone
and the people's feet
three generations later
and a hope
a breath of will
not yet extinguished by nicotine,
not yet harnessed to the begging wheel,
not yet satisfied with laughter behind a screen.
Is that enough, my brothers,
my sisters?
You've touched the stone groove
of your ancestor
you've glimpsed one second's worth
of his heart's desire
what is it you'll settle for now?
And you the alchemist of lobotomy
what shall you say of the gas released?
Did you invent Darwin
for this very moment?
Our latex shoes and our science
cannot hide us from the rock we forgot.

KULLER KULLUP

Bruce Pascoe

Kuller Kullup walked
from the stoney shoulder of Targangil
to this bend of Birrarung
spoke to all the people gathered there,
Wathaurong, Bunurong, Maap
Wurunjeri, Ganai, Taungurong,
all the people,
and he said,
the sky is falling in,
bring me poles, the longest poles,
bring me axes of sharp-edged greenstone,
for the sky is falling in.
The missionary arrived, as they usually do,
but Kuller Kullup refused to speak
while the man of god was there,
for these were the great seer's people
and his message to them was
the sky is falling in,
bring me axes, bring me poles,
together we will repair the rent
in our world.
Of course the missionary
demanded to know what was said,

as they usually do,
and for the price of a loaf of bread
to a hungry man
and a blanket,
to a woman whose child was cold,
he purchased the information
that the sky was falling in.
Oh those natives,
those children,
their savage superstitions,
Henny Penny the sky is falling in,
and soon the whole of Bearbrass
was chortling at the foolish blacks.
Some guessed, as some do, that the need for poles and axes
had a more metaphoric intent,
a more tactical thrust,
and they made sure that,
Kuller Kullup, sky master,
dream master,
was never seen again,
just in case.
How dare he assume a superior dream.
And so the dust was settled,
the gold was won,
the sheep were shorn,
banks were vaulted,

parliaments raised.
Of course the gardens
followed the rule of Kew, as you do,
no natives of course, no natives at all
for nothing in this land
could please an Englishman's hall,
except of course, the grass and gold, the beaches
a sunrise or two,
the quaintness of the kangaroo,
the docility of koala and wombat,
the duck-billed ornithorhynchus.
Exotica, unnecessary really,
when you could have a fox and a rabbit,
a trout and a blackberry,
thank you Ferdinand von Mueller,
creator of the gardens,
destroyer of rivers,
the founder of the real Australia.
Kuller Kullup

LOSS

Bruce Pascoe

If your chest quavers and you are moved to touch
Which finger would you choose?
Well, take that finger,
The one you would use to smooth
The mauve eyelid of a lover, the one you'd test the
Moisture between her lips, just before you taste,
The temperature, texture and salt of a full loving,
Take that finger
With all its memory
And draw it across the
Crown of this frail head
And watch the colour ululate,
Ululate, a throat warble, a heartsong
As the pressure of your
Loving finger depresses the napery of feather, let it progress,
As a real lover would,
To follow the curve from scalp to nape
Where the bones are so tiny,
So heartbreakingly fragile
That tears well in your eye,
Let your palm cup the body,
The perfect curve of folded flight,

The mighty power of feather and bone
Yet the lightest breeze can puff them from the page, but riffle
the page itself,
Lighter than paper,
Stronger than gravity
Weather,
Destiny,
Fate,
But your finger
Can make it shimmer like velvet,
Whisper like love.

And love can be the reverence
Of a wetted finger,
Or the regret of a finger stalling on the nape of a dead bird,
But it is still love
And only love.
Some things pass
And we have caused it,
Other things pass and there is nothing we could have done,
So love can be regret,
But regret is always love,
And regret is that the bird is gone,
Disappeared
Because we didn't love enough?

Or because the angle of the sphere is out of our control,
Also just like love.

Reflection

I was travelling through the Gariwerd Country looking at the trees altered by the old people for ceremonial purposes and I kept thinking of an azure kingfisher which I had found dead after colliding with a window the day before and so my thoughts were all about beauty, death and love ... and I'd experienced them all in one day.

BUNADA LANGUAGE

Nicole Smede

Gumea Dharawal interpretation provided by Adrian Webster

Bunada language

Born of lung, egress to mouth
rounded in hollow caverns,
our subterranean caves.

Tapered tongues, lapping ridges
in glottal patterns depart
parted lips. A vibrating hum.

Bunada language

This vital force, carried in skin
and within, a genesis of sacred stories
yarns like blood through our veins–

interconnecting
infiltration and percolation,
precipitating from ancestry.

Bunada language

These oral waves shape the land
and cascade in auditory
resonant message

enfolding meaning, cradle knowledge
and forge identity
in expressive course across the terrain.

Bunada language

Rippling outward, perpetual.
A nexus swelling and surging
in celebratory liberation.

Bunada language

Note
Bunada is a Gumea Dharawal word referring to flowing water, used here to infer the Language Flows Like a River.

WURI RISING

Nicole Smede

Dharawal interpretation provided by Jodi Edwards

Maying quiet mist
Ngulangang silently gathered
by dying ganbi

Leaving Nanggaa Gudjaga-wulawala
Gami-wulali open, yiraman chests filled
with the breath of garuwangga-wulali

Bunbal in maramal,
Mudji-wulali, burara guided
through manda wayagadi-na djibir for
the unweaned and the weary.

Warra mana guwaan
Gulgul

Returning to Ngura
Ngaba, Ngabu, boori

Gugara dja dja,
Wuri rising

PRE DAWN

Nicole Smede

In cool quiet mist
we rise silently gathered
by dying embers

Leaving sleeping babes
mouths open, warm chests filled
with the breath of dreams

Wood bowls in hand,
allies, star-guided
through thick bush seeking dew for
the unweaned and the weary.

Red Waratah
Bloodwood tree

Returning to camp
mother, grandmother, child.

Kookaburra calls
Dawn nears.

WIPED

Samuel Wagan Watson

For Martin Harrison

> *I sing the joy of wandering*
> *and the pleasure of the wandering death …*
> GUILLAUME APOLLINAIRE

I replay your voice with every word I borrow from the
dictionary,
again, and again, as it hits a page, embedded. And as the
words get harder your voice gets weaker in memory and I
fear if
I keep writing, well …

You know what will happen?
Visions of the road become overexposed in my mind, journeys
we took, words you shared with me that I tried to pass to
others,
in kind. Acoustic resonance in our textual-scapes, lyrical
tracks
and precious liner notes, that I hold close from being
consciously wiped …

OLD GHOST DOGS

Samuel Wagan Watson

Some things are beyond talking.
Not the mind, not emotions,
words will always come for them.
Perhaps the mind lives in this barrier
entirely of its own creating. You
see it the way it is, it looks back the same–
The fence, the lake, they're just there.

FROM 'A DOG BARKING', MARTIN HARRISON

A mentor once asked me if I could sense ghosts. Yes, I've been scared of the dark on many occasions where light and time can't reflect rational measures. I am no older in the night now than when I was a child; ghosts pepper shadows unevenly. You can only taste them as does my dark skin, they're just there and why should I be so afraid? I am to become one, one day soon, and then bark into the silt and yearn again to taste my breath when it was young. Future nights of my pasts-being and dog-eared visions ...

WÄŊA MARRKAPMIRR (MY BELOVED HOMELAND)

Melanie Mununggurr Williams

Dhuwal interpretations provided by Barayuwa Mununggurr

Baman' ŋarra marrtjindja
Wäŋgany gunha'yun
Barrkulil wängŋalil ŋarra marrtjindja
Ga bayŋu'yan ŋarra ruŋiyin wäŋalil gupuḏalny

Warwuyuna ŋarra yukurra dhuwal
Moṉuk'kun gapu ga dhäruk'gun ŋanharawu
Waŋganymirr ŋarra ruŋiyirrny
Yan gurriri, gurriri

Marrkapmirr Wäŋa
Ŋarra buku-wikam nhuna
Bili baḏak nhe ŋarrak galkun yukurra
Baythi ŋarra gayulny nhokal winya'yun

My feet stopped dancing
Numb to your powerful clapping beneath them,
my song fell stagnant, swampy water, mosquitoes swarmed
around me clouding my vision
the clouds turned dark, open fired pellets of purity upon me,
but I galikali

Gakarrarr–once playful nomad of salt and sand
Of mawarraki casuarinas standing guard of the land
I flew
Flew from you, from fear of the breaths I took, the milky way within my chest not yet ready to swallow
all your stars, not home enough to breathe them into your night skies
Wäŋa marrkapmirr, I fled

And with ba<u>n</u>umbirr in my eyes, lighting my darkness each time my eyelids kissed
Born Mana, always will I be, thrashing my way gracefully through waters that don't recognise,
          waters that chastise,
                    waters that dehumanise,
                              waters where I don't belong

But waiting patiently on the horizon of unknown waters sits my song
calling me home

The embrace of sleeping moon and waking sun
I thank you
For still you wait for me
Even when I fled

THE DISAPPEARING

Steve Dibirdi Hodder-Watt Bunbajee

Dreams it seems can be deprived and refuse 2 arrive like the glimpse of past lives,
Like girlfriends and wives, not gone but forgotten,
Testaments of the rotten loves linger
like the twitch of an amputated finger.
Digging in the golden river sand in the forgotten crimson spear-grass land,
Where the man spears glass in the glands of extended fam's,
gets sent 2 remand, becomes more stock 4 Z block where the clan expands,
contemporary jocks 4 the neo-millennium initiation,
a fabrication of Malcolm X Boulevard, no longer postcards,
cultural discards that retard the Tjukurrpa Dreaming, scrape the urban resin, drifting phantoms ghosting between the gums, fire drums, reserving Eccy pills and Lil Wayne stills that replace the Tyape Witchetty Grubs, the Katjarra Bush Tomato, Ingwulpa Native Tobacco, Alangwaye Wild Passionfruit.
But why should the eyes pry on them little guys when there's plenty on either side, black or white, that choose to die culturally, socially, politically, Aboriginal immigrant refugees, so please drop the unease and racial tease, U can be free 2 abscond subliminally behind a legislative

veil, but whenst U hail, the remnants fail 2 complete the detail, identities abseil in2 abysmal bliss ... what's this I am hearing, the coasts are revering but all that is echoed through the desert streets and hills is a disappearing.

OYSTER SHELL NECKLACE

Ellen van Neerven

I didn't fill the bay
or make the rocks
I didn't.
Hear Tassie's haunted
wasn't sure how I'd feel
I feel.
Water in your welcome
the clouds, the blood
water.
All feeds all
mud oysters, mutton birds
all feeds.
Parting gift
shell in your hands
now in my hands
on your neck
now on my neck.
Safe travel
with shell stringed close
heartbeat close.

GIBAM GARANDALEHN (FULL MOON)

Ellen van Neerven

Yugambeh interpretations provided by Shaun Davies, Yugambeh Library

*

Gibam garandalehn
Minyanggu giribawahla nganyi
Minyanggilehla ngaya mubu, ngi?

*

Bahbuny
Ngawragi wanyi gulgunu ngalingah
Nga giyagi 'Gumerahla wanyi ngay'

*

Guwany
Minyanggu giribawahla nganyi
Yawun nyanggai'jahra wahlugaya, ngi?

*

Gurumgan guwalehn
Gannganah ban.gehn wahlu

*

Gamay yarga
Minyanggu giribawahla nganyi
Nyumbahla nganyi nguy yugam dagarah ngay, ngi?

*

Ganggah jimi
Yugam nuwangbil
Barehbanan'galehla yarabilnu

*

Dalgah
Jagunu
Yarabih barehbanu

*

full moon–
why you keep me awake
what do you have in store for me tomorrow?

*

Nana
I wanted to speak to you in our language
and tell you I love you

*

brush-tail possum–
why you keep me awake
is the night like day to you?

*

stars broke
when they heard you died
dust fell at our feet

*

strong wind–
why you keep me awake
is it to teach me I am not alone?

*

take the feather
over the bird
dream in song

*

make music
from the land
sing in dreams

BALADJARANG

Adrian Webster

Written in Gumea Dharawal, with interpretations by Jacob Morris and Joel Deaves. With gratitude to them and their families for holding, restoring and sharing the Gumea Dharawal Language.

Naandthara cūndūlali ngia, naandtha ngiagaan
Naandthara gūrabānlali ngia, naandtha ngiagaan
Naandthara budjahnlali ngia, naandtha ngiagaan
Naandthara nudjūng ngia, naandtha ngiagaan
Naandthara Ngurra ngia, naandtha ngiagaan
Naandthara ngiagaan ngia, naadtha mugan'ndalalijaang

I look at the trees, I see myself
I look at the rocks, I see myself
I look at the water, I see myself
I look at the birds, I see myself
I look at the country, I see myself
I look at myself, I see my old people

FOREVER, FLAG

Claire G. Coleman

For Harold Thomas—Designer of the Aboriginal Flag

Forever in my blood, etched bleeding into my flesh
I remember when you wept red; the pain
Little more than an itch;
Wept, darker red than the scarlet of the ink

Without you, flag, my skin is slick, too pale
People might not know who I am
Red, yellow, black
My skin forever, flag.

The yellow, the sun, is fading
The red, the ground, the black, I
Still strong, the bloodlines.

Someone once said, 'wow, that's committed'.
Someone once said, 'you could pass as white'.
A blackfella once said, 'welcome to my Country sister'
He saw my blackfella flag first
He saw my Noongar face after.

I wear a flag
        I have it needle-stuck and inked
        Up in my skin
My skin is a flag
Without the ink
        Not flagged enough.

I say to them, 'this flag is my identity'.
I say to them, 'this ink forever'.
I say to them, 'I will die before
        I lay down my flag'.

THE LADY AT MY WINDOW

Nick Paton

Ngunawal interpretations provided by Jai Bell

Gagu Bula Gagu
Balan Mil
Garani
Gulunggaya
gaydundun
baabin
Yugu

Minya Indegee

Dhanugulanga Mil
Dhanugulanga
Gaydundun
Dhanu Ngawadjba
Indegee Mani Nganiny

Baray Dhanu
Dhanu
Yimaba Nayi Yanggu
Walu
Warumandji Walani

Wiraga Daldamanda Dhurali

Yangga Ngala
Gulanggaya

Balan
Dhanu Gudha
Nagu

Nganaga Gunanggu
Walani Gawari

Balan Nayi
Dagawinyu
Dhanugulanga
Dhanugulanga Ya Guri
Gudha Ngandin

Nadjang Maga Yarag

Dhanu
Dhanugulanga

Dhanugulanga Gudha Nganiny Dunurang
Nguraman

Ngaragalung Yarabanali

Warumandji Dhanugulanga
Djilmang

Banggur Gaway

Gulunggaya

Dhanugalunga Ganami
Indegee Nayi
Balan
Gulunggaya

Night after night,
the lady with the scary eyes,
and wiry hair,
appears at my window.
                screaming
                crying
                angry

But what did I do wrong?

Her eyes grow wider
and her indiscernible words
louder
She leans forward through the window
As I retreat to the safety of the underside of my pillow.

Faster than she came
she was gone.

You can look now
and where the window was,
there is a campfire.

The neighbour's house across the drive
reverts to a comfortable gunyah.

Song moves through the trees
and into my room.

The lady at the window smiles,
As she prepares her children
for the evening.

It is eternally calm and peaceful.

Who are these people?
Why are they camping outside my window?

The lady looks over,
and just like the setting sun–
her smile begins to fade.
Her calls to husband become desperate,
The children become frightened.

Mother smothers the fire and prepares for battle.

She uses instinct
to hide herself.

She places the children under bark.
Using the dark cover of night,

The villains arrive

With their muskets
and mongrels muted.

And there she is again at my window.
          silent

Now showered in tears of red.

Closing my eyes never ails.

Her image burns my consciousness–
I remain staring
at the lady
at my window.

CONDUIT

Nick Paton

Ngunawal interpretations provided by Jai Bell

Gulunggaya Ngining Bilbi Nadjang Daoure Indegee Dhari
  Dhawura
Indegee Gulunggaya Bayang Dhanu Indegee–
Gawar Mangga
Gawar

Indegee Gulunggaya Mil Daoure

Gulunggaya Mara–
Dhanugulanga Gunanggu
Dhanugulanga Ngurumbang

Indegee Gulunggaya Dambalinyi

Indegee Gulunggaya Gawar Minga

Nguna Minya Yimaba Bula Ganan
Nadjang Daoure Dhuni
Indegee

Bunima
Dhanu Dhuniyang Indegee
Djaan Mara–

Yimaba Ganan Wandiny Yimaba Djaan
Dhanu Dhuniyang

Banggi Indegee Gulunggaya Mara Ganan Nadjang Daoure

My feet are covered in dirt from Mother Earth as I stand still
on her Country.
I use my body as conduit as she begins to fill me–
with a heartfelt message,
with utmost love,

I open my eyes to the truth inscribed in the earth

My hands uncover the stories–
her people
her places

I use my mind like a justice scale
and endeavour to weigh up the facts–
with incriminating evidence,
with undeniable proof

I close my heart to the trauma etched upon page
I can't comprehend this hurt

This is what you need to know
Mother Earth will say
as I become threadbare

Winds of change
she tells me
are already on the way–

You'll know when you're ready
She says

Over thick skin I rub my hands
and listen deeply to Mother Country.

LA – PA

Brenda Saunders

I remember taking the tram to 'the Loop'
on those fishing days with Dad. Crowds
on their way to see the 'Snake Men' scaring
all the kids, uncles selling boomerangs.
Shy moments with aunties living in shacks
along the bay. Cousins. Big boys too busy
for the small girl under their feet
waiting for the main event at the jetty.
I watched them dive for silver, gliding
through seaweed, sleek bodies shadowy
in the underwater sun. They showed no fear
of barnacles as they surfaced under the steps
Shaking the water from their dark curls
the bounty caught between white teeth.

Lapa: La Perouse, Botany Bay. Former Aboriginal Reserve

The Loop: circular tram terminus

THE BATHURST PLAIN

Brenda Saunders

'Latest Discoveries: fine open country ... with wooded plains reminiscent of an Englishman's Estate'
'The Expeditions of Major Mitchell', State Library of NSW

We watched them come with new ideas for change, create
'a green and pleasant land' on dusty plains, clear our wildlife
for sport or game. They brought Red coats, mulled wine.
Hounds for the English hunt, chasing a fox on the run.
Smoothed the outcrops, straightened our snaky trails
for the shortest route to town. Cleared forests, squared
the land into parcels bound with wire. They drove sheep
onto patchy runs, planted seed in a land with no seasons.
They gave new names to our rivers and creeks. New laws
defied our old beliefs, sent starving families drifting
off Country. Skirmishes turning the tribe in on itself
knowing the white man had come to stay.

PASSAGE OF TIME

Eric Avery

De Arco
summer of content
assonance
radiating through
Passage of time
music terms
moving through
mists papilla reborn
into a new skin torn
out of pages forlorn
the music of our ancestors in lines
drawings recordings
songs need physical reality
to papilla wakanha
moving through mists
deciphering reality
through a different sense
the mists of the past come back to cleanse
to heal to mend
Wakaymali
to sing to cause to dance
Wakanhawinanga
dances of listening

listening to truth
through our songs and stories
the land is our proof
of our resilience
in our songs we cry
out to the sky
the land reflected in our eyes
Passage of time
Passage of Blood
hears and echoes throughout the bay
can you live when faced by death
beat of the heart created from
heat in our lungs
like the time in our sleep
when we dream of azure days
out of pain and deceit
violins sound like drums in this cosmopolitan piece
  composed out of here
Passage of time.

FOR THE YOUNG

Celestine Rowe

It's time for our young people to rise
Take the fight laid before us
Let's rise to the challenges
We fight against depression, oppression, suicide
Genocide, displacement, child rights
They say we're equal
We bleed the same
But we're not treated the same
In our land it's not the same
We're made to feel like it's our fault
History hidden behind government cloak
Truth hidden behind exaggerated lies
Of what was but we know
We're still living it
Belongs to us
Brothers and sisters and uncles and aunties
Still falling, dying to the system.
Let's rise to the occasion
Let's tell the world our government system's failing
To the people that were here first
Too many generations displaced and hurt
We stand up because we should
Our people still hurt

For our mob for the voices mistook
We fight for reasons anyone with understanding cannot stand
They say we're equal
Then when
Was it the 1967 referendum?
Then if so, why haven't we been included in the government's
so-called constitution
And why we still gotta be recognised
In white eyes racist eyes
Everybody understands but them, rednecks.
We fight for the little babies taken away
In this day and age
We cry, we shed tears for them
Because I imagine it could have been mine.
I stand up for the good ones
The families who fight to keep it strong.
Still them government think they're doing justice
A poor mother on welfare has no justice
Her baby gets taken away
Another fight before her lays
Instead of fighting the system
She is fighting for her life
Attempted suicide.
Who are we supposed to be when it's all ripped up for greed
We have no more stories
Them hundred year leases with them all the so-called glories

What about my brothers at Bush
That want to work and teach the young how the world's
  supposed to be.
They get sent away from home
And everything is not as glorious as portrayed.
This was and always will be Aboriginal land.

THE WOUNDED BRAVE

Joel Davison

Written partially in Gadigal, with interpretations by Joel

Bayawurradyangun, djirrundyangun
We are all wounded, we all fear
Ngabay midyungngunbuni ngaliya
Together, you and I, we will heal

Narangla ngaramila, ganunigang bayawurra ngalawabuni
Be humble and listen, old wounds be still
munurudyawawingun ngaliya
We have forgotten our friends
giyara duwabilidya
their names hidden from us
manawariwawingunla gurra wugulgu
let us find them once more

Buraga! Baya, buruga!
Rise! Voices and hands!
Yanma baru, yanma bulbuwul
Move fast and move strong
naminmamila nugbady, dunga ngyinigai migal
Show your love and shed your tears
Yilabara, badjamibuni, midyungmibuni
Today, do not harm, but mend

Bayawurradyangun, djirrundyangun
We are all wounded, we all fear

Dyarrbabangunbuni ngimagay
We will never grow weary or let our fire burn out
Burawangunla, naminmawawingun dara
Let's move upward and show our teeth
Yanangunla, barayangunla mari bula
Let's move together and sing out loud
Naawala, mimugurubuni, yanagn un, ngyinarigai gana
  manuwi
Look, do not close your eyes, we walk together, with feet on
  fire

MY CITY

Joel Davison

Written partially in Gadigal, with interpretations by Joel

A city stands on ancestral
  lands
Yagu, winima

Now, close

I found a void where it is
  made perfect

Passing as white, painted up
  white,
in white rabbit
laughing at white canvas

Painted white, white,
painted white and mourning,
we laughed hysterically

Dabuwamili, dyirra, mubi
Badiyangun

Ignited my life and my love

You set my heart on fire

Ngaya butbut Gunamamiwa

A city stands on my ancestral
lands
My hands whiter than my
ancestor's hands
My city stands on my
ancestral lands

Gamarabu, guwugu,
barrabugu, barrabuwari,
darimi

Today, now, tomorrow,
the day after tomorrow,
for a long time

My city

LONGING, WANTING

Stiff Gins

Longing, Wanting
My edge, a blade
Slice through air, slice through air
No breath, no rain
Stay in wait and wait to fade away

Wanting, longing for
That arm, that fingernail

My edge, a blade
No breath, no rain
Stay in wait and wait to fade away

Wanting, longing for
That arm that fingernail
Wanting, longing
That arm that fingernail
My edge is a blade of steel
Revered I reveal a man of pride
I hang proud at his side
I began again and again
With hand, finger, nail

Etched in fine line
Wood, tooth, sinew, shell and twine
Combine to launch and strike
I kill divided evermore through time
I lie, wait and wail
His hand, finger, nail

Wanting, longing
That arm, that fingernail
Wanting, longing for
That arm, that fingernail
longing for ...

REMNANT

Ryan Prehn

remnant /rɛmnənt/ *noun*

1. a part or quantity that is left after the greater part has been used, removed, or destroyed.

    i. a piece of cloth left when the greater part has been used or sold.

    ii. a surviving trace.

one of the baluk, this old river red
rooted neath the spear grass
she fights, still
against tender regression
transient demise

eco-virgin, Chronos, comes
surfaces for sour air
shortness of breath
lasting centuries
youse gonna eat that?

gaseous slobbering
on composted history
that ruminates, splinters,

'dieback is for faggots'–
a colonial time-stamp

and muyan remembers
hotly, biel and ballee smoke
the crow, Waang,
watches this young fire
welcome to country

ignore the stagnant, white reek
that interrupts cathartic embrace
for these old girls
hug your very needs
how does that feel, sugar?

obvious and heavy
forced, despite all wants
later it would be better
today might have been special
another day promising
with that easy and obvious love
and casual manner, soon
it would be better
worse, also
the burden you've to inherit
is no easier than it has been

writ into your rings
and forced upon our backs
somehow, with love

Note
Definition from lexico.com
A Koori Smoking Ceremony often accompanies a Welcome to Country.
Three plants are used in the smoking burn:
muyan–silver wattle (symbolic of Elders)
ballee–cherry ballart (symbolic of youth)
biel–river red gum (symbolic of entire community and its access to Country)
This smoke is a physical merge of the old and the new. Visitors to Country pass through the smoke and are cleansed, protected, and discouraged of ill intent.

'Remnant' recognises slurs as being a colonial introduction into these lands. 'Composted History' is the result of the colonial project, that splinters realities into untruths through cultural whitewashing. There is much story (and academia) that tells us gender fluidity and diverse sexualities have existed on this continent in plural forms prior to the colonial dismantling of culture and genocide of our peoples, and there is a continuation of some of these diversities today. However, the injection of Christianity into Australia through the missionaries came gifted with the enduring legacies of chronic homophobia and toxic masculinities (along with many others), and that the idea that difference equates deficit. Throughout 'Remnant' I use italicized wording for the 'voices of others'. This voice is the product of composted history, and whose very toxicity causes, or is, the dieback that the remnant tree must fight against. So colonial is the blindness to look at an old, dying tree and only recognise its utility as chopped wood, rather than as both a part and product of the world around it.

CALBUNYAS INITIATION

Kaitlen Wellington

Gumea Dharawal interpretation provided by Jacob Morris and Adrian Webster

climbin djera
calbunya shows itself
stalkin on twigs and leaves
makin a point to get my attention
sayin gone go learn language now

come day
trek to bundanon
da old goodjie

learnin new knowledge
from brotha boy
calbunya master of language
it taught us aye
da old people
in old days
how to gum

we gali for calbunya
boorais step to clapsticks
nurri
nurri
nurri

i and brotha boy connect bloodlines
his ngubu
and my baabaa coomie
a few generations back
are first cousins
carpenter line

dis aint no coincidence
i am meant to be ere
ancestors
yes dey guindin me

still morange tho
and still unsure
i go out culburra beach
walkin my track
uh whats dat
der in da bush

calbunya
 whip once
whip bulla
 sayin yes you learn your language daught

bless I been askin to learn language
    linkin in with sista girl has been the best thing

the journey has just begun
 long way to go now but I cant back out
cause when ya told to do somethin
 you do it
cause knowledge is power
 and with power comes responsibility

SPIRITS HOPE

Kaitlen Wellington

Gumea Dharawal interpretation provided by Jacob Morris and Adrian Webster

Ngubu
Ngubumarra
Niga miru
Buradja Nia
As we heal

Grandmother
Mother
I dream
Tomorrow good
As we heal

EYES OF FEELING

Lionel G. Fogarty

In = meek
My feelins have not change
One with the murri
And we are alone
My feelins are a thought
Of sad past life
Yet i'm words without words
My feelins are mind
Disregarding me i found
My love lies race above
Those feelins done
We were born to fight
My feelins have not eyes have feeling

WASTE OR WORSE

Lionel G. Fogarty

Alternative on trustees with our Australia
Won't do, won't do?
Progressive is becoming confusing at times
Absorb an external protest
My and our mates.
Recruitment to blackfella systems
Is punching old equilibriums.
Candidates; experimental
Available college racists
Degrees by not teaching it
In re-evaluating research material
Is bad schools; bad for children
Or splendid and responsive
To keep and ancient drugs training.
Yes; yes. Topics are affiliated by
Counterinsurgency mentality.
Embattled by national educating
Impatient implications.
These are to half our future.
Australia is behind the styles
Australia can be in our styles.
Sharply; the substitute is specific
We have to be

Conventional wine academics.
Look at Aboriginals
Kaleidoscope he'll tell you
You going exactly the wrong
Disciplinary way.
Restoration we've got to aim for
Compulsory and trivial
Feeble and capricious efforts
Australia can create dignity.
Contempt is largely made on our people
Just to worsen it's up-spirit
Into spirit.
Can you rationalise that?

MUDJIS AND YILIMAN

Lyndsay Urquhart

Written with Dharawal, Dhurga and Darumba interpretations provided by Vikki Parsley and Jodi Edwards

Reach to the birrung, if you dare
for our ancestors they live there
Yukon Guwin
Ngura bugiya
232 years of bugiya have failed you
Ngaa mujis, guwin in a garawanga,
Jumping into the dilwan
Gurguma, barnun, yilma, marwdi yabun yukon guwin
Gagamari, bidiga, buldayn, djaja, gurbin, mudji
Ngaa nabu now on the gayan garabang
Ngaa nabu, mujis yangga-na, and gali for you
Ngaa gadu bana from their mabura
Ngura duduwa calling, waiting
Under the cross
Ngaa ganbi burning, and the yiliman sharpening.

Reach to the stars, if you dare
For our ancestors they live there
speak up spirits of the dead
I hear yesterday
232 years of yesterday have failed you
I see friends, spirits of the dead in a dream
Jumping into the sunset
Westerly wind, north-easterly wind, southerly wind, easterly wind speak up for the spirits of the dead
Cleverman, grandmother, grandfather, cousin, friend
I see your family now all on the big rock
I see your family friends singing and dancing for you
I see the ocean water from their eyes
I hear the whip bird, calling, waiting
under the cross
I see fire burning, and the spears sharpening.

BAN MAGANINDADJYANG (MY OLD PEOPLE DONE)

Jacob Morris

Written in Gumea Dharawal, with interpretations by Jacob

Waagl Ngura Ngiagaang, Ban Gili Maganindadjyang
Naantharra Ngura Ngiagaang, Ban Gili Maganindadjyang
Gunama Ngura Ngiagaang, Ban Gili Maganindadjyang
Yanggam Ngura Ngiagaang, Ban Gili Maganindadjyang
Krabre Ngura Ngiagaang, Ban Gili Maganindadjyang
Nguboodji Ngura Ngiagaang, Ban Gili Maganindadjyang

I travel Country, like my Old People done
I see the Country, like my Old People done
I burn Country, like my Old People done
I sing Country, like my Old People done
I dance for Country, like my Old People done
I love Country, like my Old People done

DISCONNECTION

Kirli Saunders

Gundungurra interpretations provided by Trish Levett and Aunty Val Mulcahy

Goodjahgah
nga gamiri ngyini mundu
empty spaces
for gummuang words to fill
and stretch your guri
for the pialla and their voices

nga gamiri your
trembling limbs ache to shake
in tangara
and hear your lungs as they gasp yoongaba

nga feel your
body sans
burrungilling
yabbun
and secret

and know that
it has been grown
with roots wrenched
from the daoure that cradled them

and nga taste the hunger
ngyini do
to know the parts of yourself
to feel yurwang

when your
Duwi has been taken

Little one,
I see you mouth empty spaces
for a mother's words to fill
and stretch your ears
for the stories and their voices

I watch your trembling limbs
ache to shake
in dance
and hear your lungs
as they gasp with songs unknown

I feel your
body sans
spirit,
ceremony
and secret

and know that
it has been grown
with rots
wrenched
from the earth
that cradled them

and I taste the hunger
you do
to know the parts of yourself
to feel at home

when your
Dreaming has been taken

MOTHER

Kirli Saunders

Mother,
I've spent hours now
searching for myself
in the symmetry of your skin
in the blues and greens of your depths.

I watch the sand dance to your tides,
And see the tannins,
like tea
tessellate upon your earthy limbs.

I find my feet in the foot holes
of our people,
long gone now

and I know
that this
is where I belong.

HARD LEARNING

Kirli Saunders

For Poetry in First Languages Arrernte leaders Janette, Declan and Carmel

Curtained off from
all known things
were lessons
enshrined in sand–
wisdom carved out
the old way,
with fingertips to Red Earth
in salt bush scrub,
a fire crackling close by

Lessons
in Arrernte
of sparkling Yipirinya Dreaming–
softly spoken by an Elder
in the cold of winter
as rain clouds formed
over chapped ranges

Wisdom
that could only be told
as the drought broke,
in the company of

coolibahs and brumbies
children and healers,
to a saltwater woman
far from home–
who needed to hear it.

BRIDGE OVER THE RIVER MEMORY

Jeanine Leane

Prince Alfred Bridge, Gundagai

When I come back I remember it has
been a long time.
Long time passing since
I came back along this track to Gundagai–
town of my childhood.
There are many ghosts–I hear
their voices.

I stand on a solid red-gum bridge–the
longest wooden bridge in the world.
The Irish nuns told me this on a good
day under the gothic arches in the convent
on the hill where I learnt about Australian history.
This continent, Australia, is a young country,
they told us. *The history of this place is very*
short–shortest in the world!
They'd seen the world–the nuns.
Maps were pinned on the wall to show
how far they'd travelled to spread the word.
I'd only seen my Country.
The longest bridge and the shortest history–
that's what I learnt.

Prince Alfred Bridge they called it–built
last century–by the pioneers as
they opened up the lands for progress.
Our teachers said so.
How many river gums were felled? What
were their names before they were rearranged
across the river–once their life blood.
What was their history?
My Grandmother said this place is old.
She said my teachers don't know the stories.
I listened.
On a bad day you could be beaten
for asking the wrong questions about
the short history and the long bridge.
At school I learnt to hold my tongue.

The water under the bridge ripples over
my memory now. The bend of the
Murrumbidgee–a deep archive–
flows steady and slow.
I walk on the bridge and I remember how
long it used to take to cross on my little
legs clinging tight to the side rail as huge
wheat and wool trucks thundered over the
ancient planks laden with the wealth
of the nation.

Sometimes the river rose so high it swallowed
the bridge and the town. Short history almost
washed away by higher, older tides.
No trucks now. The bridge long ago closed–
steel and concrete girders bypass the town.
The wealth of the nation rumbles down
different roads.

On the other side I look back across
the flood plains. The old stone convent on
the hill is empty.
I come back after seeing the world.
I hear my Grandmother again.
The bridge is short now.
But this history of place is still
deep and long.

NGINHA-GULIA NYIANG—THESE WORDS

Jeanine Leane

Wiradjuri interpretations provided by Aunty Elaine Lomas

These words cry out and I hear them–learn to mould
and shape them like clay.
There should have been a time for such words.
for this word–'Nginha Nyiang'
And a word for such time Guwayu

How clunky these are as I first stumble over them.
Grappling like the child I should have been when I first
felt them–'Winungah Dilinyi', Sang them–'Babiyi',
Spoke them–'yayi'

Now my clumsy tongue struggles over each new
syllable my Country 'Ngurambang' gives me.

Each one I want to devour like the sweetest thing.
'Wiluray Bang Gula-dhayi' I ever tasted.
I want to suck every shred of the marrow
'Dundumbirra' from each solid sound.
I want to swallow it whole 'Darra-Marra'
to know what it is to eat for the first time
I want to feel like the child born to these words
'Gudha Dhurrinya Nginha Nyiang'

YANHA-MAM-BIRRA—RELEASE

Jeanine Leane

Wiradjuri interpretations provided by Aunty Elaine Lomas

The space of my emptiness is a chasm so deep so wide
I'll fall to endless nothing without your words to cross it.

I have starved for you to feed my soul nourish my
blood to strengthen my bones, Ngadhi Bagurany
dhabul (ngadhi bugaray darbhul)
I have craved for the taste of your sound on my
parched lips the drip-drop of your coolness on my
parched palette. dulba nginhu balaba nganda-birra
mugumaga (mucu maga)
Ached for you to speak to sing to sound to shout
release your syllables to the air that I can breathe you
drink you grasp you. murun-wiginya nyal,
yirba-dharra nyal, mulgamarra nyal.
My tongue thick–a heavy cringing prisoner bashed
and battered by two hundred and thirty years of
colonial submission stalls stubborn over your form.
For too long my mouth paid lip-service to English
been a slave to grammar prisoner to punctuation
handmaiden to pronunciations servant of prim
proper and poise.

Life sentence lifted my tongue can liberate my heart
with these words from you
I am Wiradjuri ... Badhu Wiradjuri
I am proud ... Badhu Dyiramadilinya
I am here ... Badhu Nginha

NURAMBANG YALI—
COUNTRY SPEAKS

Jeanine Leane

Wiradjuri interpretations provided by Aunty Elaine Lomas

It's been too long since I sat on granite in my
Country and thought

Too many years since I breathed this air–
Bunyi-ng–ganha
Felt this dirt–Ngamanhi Dhaagun
Smelt this dust–Budha–nhi Bunan

Listened for the sounds of her words that say
'Balandha–dhuraay Bumal-ayi-nya Wumbay
abuny (yaboing)' –History does not have the
first claim. Nor the last word.
Nghindhi yarra dhalanbul ngiyanhi gin gu
'You can speak us now!'

BANGGANG CŪNDŪ (OLD TREE)

Joel Deaves

Poem is written in Gumea Dharawal, with interpretations by Joel

Nandhirra ngundāmurrajāng ngala walbūgging ngia
Nandhirra ngundāmurrajāng ngallaēnmarri
  māndijāngwūlunyun ngia
Ngaradha yanggamarri ngūranyaga ngia
Wadgamānya ngundāmurrajāng būlwūlpa galina
Ngaradha jerralali yagiabilla ngia
Būwnj ngurajāng dharundharung gilinya ngia
Nandhirra burungalaligū gūdjielalinya ngia
Nandhirra murrawal garangama ngūrajang ngia
Ngaradha bulwarinya ngia
Ngaradha būlmbillanya ngia
Būwnj dūgeri ngia
Nandhirra ngundāmurrajāng daran:ba djillnadjānnya ngia
Nandhirra ngundāmurrajāng būlwūlwiliabilla ngia
Nandhirra ngūrajāng dharandharung gillinya ngia

I see the people live at peace
I see the people share their meat
I heard the singing on the land
That made the people strong and dance
I heard the stories told again and again
I remember the country always the same
I see the boats come towards the camps
I see other people steal the land
I heard the falling
I heard the fighting
I remember crying
I see the people go through the pain
I see the people become strong again
I see the country always the same

MOTHERS LOST SONG

Maureen O'Keefe

Mothers has disappeared never to be sung again. So who will sing mothers song this song is ancient as the land itself. Mothers song has disappeared like a whisper in the wind. Through sands of time this song echoed through a thousand years. It's to me but a fading memory but I still hear her singing in the wind. Her singing echoing through the desert I see her in my dreams singing to me she sings of long ago when the earth was young this beautiful gifted woman the singer of songs she tells about the spirit woman the giver of this beautiful song. She says she is from the sky where the stars twinkle at night she dances on the milky way slowly floating down to earth she gave mother this song who could sing as beautifully as she. So who will sing mothers song. If I could turn back time just to hear her sing to me. A beautiful song never to be sung mothers song is lost. Erased by the winds of changes nothing but a whisper in the wind a faint whisper in the distance. Mothers song carried away into the distance. Maybe the wind will bring a new song please whisper these songs to me I want to hear it. The only singing I hear in the desert is the rustling of leaves singing of the birds the drone of the noisy cicadas the howling of the dingoes the hooting of the desert owl and the sound of crickets the sound of the desert where mothers song once echoed. Her singing carried off by the desert wind into the distance mothers song has disappeared into the wind.

KOOLARK—HOME

Daniel Hansen

From the woodlands to the Sclerophyll,
Of the Eucalypt Forests I know,
Within the air I can certainly feel,
A benevolence which resembles that of Home.

'Nganyang Kwoorl Daniel Murray Hansen,
Ngany Yoorl Koorl Ballardong Boodjar
Koolarngwetta Wadjuk Boodjar.'

'My Name is Daniel Murray Hansen,
I come from Ballardong Country,
Born Wadjuk Country.'

'Ngany Kooditj Alimagan Ngany,
Dabakan Koorliny Kaada Boodjar.'
'I think as I
Walk slowly across country.'

'Ngalak Katitdj Ngalang Maya,
Ngalak Katitdj Ngalang Boodjar.'
'We know our place,
We know our Land.'
The Kings Land.

The final resting place of the Waargul spirit,
Where the royalty of the Nyoongar people would hold their
  Corroborees
The most sacred of land.

Where cleanliness is next to Godliness.
And everything is kept spotless 24/7.
Which is why my people have always given the Blessing
of cleanliness to the Boodjar we Respect,
Always leaving our camping spots cleaner than when we
  entered the area,
Everywhere we declared,
'Nyanlang Koolark.'
'Our Home.'

AFTER VIEWING THE CARVED TREES EXHIBITION

Gayle Kennedy

Arborglyphs, Dendroglyphs
These are the scientific words
The white man uses to describe
Our tree writing, the sophisticated hieroglyphics
Of an ancient culture, an ancient civilisation
These are the words used to describe
The arboreal classrooms on which
Our ceremonies & laws were writ large
The sweat & blood of the carvers impregnating
The DNA of our people into the
Limbs of the sapwood and heartwood
That lined the pathway of learning
For the young warriors & their teachers

Did giving them these cold, hard words
Calling them the tree carvings of a primitive people,
Make it easier for the scientist,
The anthropologist, the land coveter
To rip them from their belonging place?
To destroy the warriors' classrooms or
Desecrate the graves of our lost ancestors?

Did they make it easier to rip
The memorial trees carved with
All the knowledge needed to
Provide a pathway for the
Spirit of the lost hero to
Find his way to the sky world?
Did they not see the rounded,
Almost fecund mound that was
The final resting place of someone
Whose loss caused such grief,
Much keening, wailing, & self inflicted
Physical pain to replace the deep
Agony of mourning?

Did those words blind them to the
Ancient knowledge contained
In the chevrons, the curvilinear, the scrolls?
Did they make them easy for people
To transplant them to their backyards
To stand beside the roses & grevilleas
And the transplanted weeds
Watered, & cut and tortured & tamed
Into green blankets to disguise the dust & earth
Of a land they could never really own?
Did they give them carte blanche
To place the trees in the dark, dank bowels of museums,

Those grand stone buildings, receivers of stolen goods
Repositories of not just ours
But other peoples' plundered cultures?

And our people, herded onto missions,
Their possum skin cloaks & kangaroo rugs
Replaced by burlap, hessian & calico
Their bush food by flour, sugar & tea and
Their spirits, their beliefs by the single god
Of the conquering peoples?
Did they dream of the Yammunyamun?
The impending initiation?
The invitations sent near & far
The feasting, the dancing, the singing?
Did they long for the comfort of their own ceremonies?
Their own way of being now gone and now
Replaced by the unfamiliar bought by
Ships, and bullock drays and horses?

And do we mob, the ancestors of
The carvers, the teachers, the initiated
Take comfort from the return of our trees
or from the revelation of our lost
And forgotten ceremony
Or from the photos in black & white & faded sepia
Of a world and ways now gone?

Do we celebrate?
Do we own our anger
Or do we forgive?
Or do we let the tears
Fall where they may?

CONTRIBUTORS

Evelyn Araluen is the co-editor of *Overland* and an award-winning poet, writer, educator and researcher who has been working with Indigenous literatures at the University of Sydney. Her work has won the Nakata Brophy Prize for Young Indigenous Writers, the *Overland* Judith Wright Poetry Prize and a Wheeler Centre Next Chapter Fellowship. Born, raised and writing in Dharug country, she is a Bundjalung descendant.

Eric Avery is a Ngiyampaa, Yuin, Bandgalang and Gumbangirr artist. As part of his practice Eric plays the violin, dances and composes music. Working with his family's custodial songs he seeks to revive and continue on an age-old legacy–continuing the tradition of singing in his tribe–utilising his talents to combine and create an experience of his people's culture.

Ethan Bell is a Wallabalooa man from the Ngunawal Nation. He is an emerging artist and student based in Campbelltown, Sydney. Ethan's practice is storytelling, drawing from his love of hip-hop. Ethan writes poetry in hopes to give insight into his life.

John 'Muk Muk' Burke was born in Narrandera in 1946 and his mother was the daughter of a resident of Warangesda Mission at Darlington Point, New South Wales. His father was of Irish heritage. Because of his fair skin, identification as Wiradjuri has been a long-time battle. Because of his position on the sexual spectrum, John has taken ages to be comfortable with what is clearly a non-binary situation. Both ethnicity and sexuality are arguably the most fraught dimensions humans deal with. John dearly hopes this book will communicate to many persons and, indeed, their many selves.

Ali Cobby Eckermann's first collection *little bit long time* was written in the desert and launched her literary career in 2009. In 2013 Ali toured Ireland as the Australian Poetry Ambassador and won the Kenneth Slessor Prize for Poetry and Book of the Year (NSW) for *Ruby Moonlight* (Magabala Books), a verse novel. In 2014 Ali was the inaugural recipient of the Tungkunungka Pintyanthi Fellowship at Adelaide Writers Week, and the first Aboriginal Australian writer to attend the International Writing Program at University of Iowa. In 2017 Ali received a Windham-Campbell Award for Poetry from Yale University, USA.

Claire G. Coleman is a Wirlomin Noongar woman whose ancestral country is on the south coast of Western Australia. Her novel *Terra Nullius* was published by Hachette (Australia) and Small Beer Press (USA), she won the black&write! Fellowship and a Norma K. Hemming Award and was short-listed for the Stella Prize and the Aurealis Science Fiction

Award. She writes poetry, short fiction and essay and has been published in the *Saturday Paper*, the *Guardian*, *Meanjin*, *Australian Poetry*, *Art Collector*, the *ABC*, *Griffith Review*, *Overland*, *Timothy McSweeny's Quarterly Concern* and many others. *The Old Lie* (Hachette, 2019) is her second novel.

Paul Collis is a Barkindji person, born in Bourke, New South Wales. He is a writer of poetry and prose and is an early-career academic living in Canberra and teaching creative writing at University of Canberra. In 2016 his novel *Dancing Home* won the David Unaipon Award for a previously unpublished Indigenous author, and in 2018 *Dancing Home* was awarded the ACT Book of the Year.

Joel Davison is a Sydney Aboriginal (Gadigal) man who was recently given an opportunity to learn and teach the Sydney Aboriginal language at the Sydney Festival. Drawing on varied experience at the education department of the Royal Botanic Gardens, Sydney, as a web developer at an Indigenous media business, Ngakkan Nyaagu, and as a robotics analyst at Commonwealth Bank, Joel believes that language is a strong component of a wholesome understanding of Aboriginal culture, heritage and history.

Joel Deaves is a Gumea Dharawal man and Dharumba Dhurga descendant from the Yuin people. Joel began learning language from his uncle and, with his cousin Jacob, set a path on which he hasn't looked back. From the learning of his language, Joel's passion grew for continuing and returning his culture, not just for him but for his family as well. In his spare time Joel is with family, speaking and restoring the Gumea Dharawal language with Jacob Morris and Adrian Webster or walking on Yuin Country with his cousins, continuing their connection to the land just as their old people did. Joel has been commissioned for the Poetry in First Languages project for Red Room Poetry.

Lionel G. Fogarty is a Yugambeh man and was born on Wakka Wakka land in South Western Queensland near Murgon on a 'punishment reserve' outside Cherbourg. Throughout the 1970s, he worked as an activist for Aboriginal Land Rights and protesting Aboriginal deaths in custody. He has published numerous collections of poetry, including the award-winning *Connection Requital, Mogwie-Idan: Stories of the land*, and *Eelahroo (Long Ago) Nyah (Looking) Mobo-Mobo (Future).*

Declan Furber Gillick is an Arrernte playwright, artist, educator, performer and musician with Aboriginal and Irish-Anglo ancestry. His works include the multi-award-winning play *Bighouse Dreaming* and *Scar Trees,* a theatre-as-education play commissioned by Ilbijerri Theatre Company. Declan has had prose, poetry and essays published by Affirm Press,

Southerly, Centre For Indigenous Story and Red Room Poetry. He is working on a new play for Melbourne Theatre Company, where he is a resident writer in their Next Stage program.

My name is **Daniel Hansen** and I am a 30-year-old Nyoongar writer from Armadale, Perth. I started to write poems when I was younger but have now moved on to writing more deeply involved poems and short stories. I am a father of three, two boisterous sons plus a gorgeous attitude-filled daughter. I started writing 20 years ago when I was 11 and first heard Eminem's album *The Marshall Mathers LP* and fell in love with hip-hop, which is another form of poetry. After studying Tupac's outlook on poetry, writing and expression of self I was able to refine my craft. Writing has helped me through hard times and I owe a lot to it. I like to incorporate my belief in Spirit and Dreamtime that I have experienced through my life into my writing.

Matthew Heffernan is an Indigenous/Irish man, who was introduced to poetry through song writing and particularly hip-hop culture. Matthew has performed as a rapper in a variety of settings across the Northern Territory and Australia, and now draws on the idiosyncrasies of this art form as a basis for all his writing. Hailing from Alice Springs but calling Darwin home, Matthew writes from the perspective of love, curiosity and strength.

Steve Dibirdi Hodder-Watt Bunbajee is a Lardil man with English heritage and has been writing poetry and spoken word rhymes in Mparntwe / Alice Springs since 2000. He has performed and spoken at events including the National Young Writers' Festival, Melbourne Emerging Writers' Festival, Wordstorm NT Writers' Festival and has also worked on poetry and hip-hop in remote Aboriginal communities in the Northern Territory and Queensland, including Aurukun, Doomadgee, Warakurna, Warburton, Warnan and Mparntwe. After 30 years on Central Arrernte Country, in 2015 he returned to the sea-country homelands of the Lardil peoples on the Aboriginal island Gununa, known colonially as Mornington Island.

Brisbane-born **Yvette Holt** heralds from the Bidjara, Yiman and Wakaman Nations of Queensland. She is a multi-award-winning poet, essayist, editor, stand-up comedienne, academic and photographer of erotic desert femin_artistry discoursed through colonial votive imagery. Her works have been published, reviewed, anthologised, digitalised and translated in print and online. Yvette has lived and worked in the Central Australian deserts for more than ten years.

Jeanine Leane is a Wiradjuri writer, poet and academic from south-west New South Wales. Her first volume of poetry, *Dark Secrets After Dreaming: A.D. 1887–1961* (Presspress,

2010) won the 2010 Scanlon Prize for Indigenous Poetry and her first novel, *Purple Threads* (UQP), won the David Unaipon Award for an unpublished Indigenous writer in 2010. Her poetry and short stories have been published in *Hecate: An Interdisciplinary Journal of Women's Liberation, Journal of the European Association for Studies of Australia, Journal for the Association of Australian Literary Studies, Australian Poetry Journal, Antipodes, Overland, Best Australian Poems, Lifted Brow, Southerly* and *Australian Book Review.* In 2017 Jeanine was the winner of the University of Canberra Aboriginal and Torres Strait Islander Poetry Prize, and she has twice been the winner of the Oodgeroo Noonuccal Poetry Prize (2017, 2019). In 2018 she was shortlisted for the Australian Catholic University National Poetry Prize. Her poetry also features in art exhibitions, installations, promotional material and public transport. Jeanine's second volume of poetry, *Walk Back Over*, was released in 2018 by Cordite Books. In 2019 Jeanine was the recipient of the Red Room Poetry Fellowship. She has published widely in the area of Aboriginal literature, writing otherness and creative non-fiction poetry and prose. Jeanine is the recipient of an Australia Research Council grant on Aboriginal literature: *Aboriginal Writing: Shaping the literary and cultural history of Australia, since 1988.* She teaches creative writing and Aboriginal literature at the University of Melbourne.

Carissa Lee is a Wemba-Wemba and Noongar actor and writer based in Melbourne. Having graduated with her acting degree from Flinders University Drama Centre, Carissa is undertaking her PhD in Indigenous theatre through the University of Melbourne. Carissa's writing has featured in Witness Performance, Book Riot, Lip Mag, ArtsHub, IndigenousX and Junkee.

Gayle Kennedy is from the New South Wales Ngiyaampa Nation. Her poetry collection *Koori Girl Goes Shoppin'* was shortlisted in 2005 for the David Unaipon Award. Gayle won the award in 2006 with *Me, Antman & Fleabag*, which was subsequently published by UQP in 2007. Gayle has published 11 children's books with Oxford University Press, and articles and poems in national and international publications.

Lola McKickett is a Ballardong, Whadjuk yok, born to Clarence and Enid Kickett (nee Hayden). Lola has returned to her writing after many years of solace and finds poetry to be particularly therapeutic. Thanks to daughter Esther (Yabini Kickett) for making this possible.

Jacob Morris is a Gumea-Dharawal Ngundah of the Yuin Murring from the south-east coast of New South Wales. Jacob's great-grandmother Lena Chapman was one of the last

Dharawal speakers from the South Coast. She kept language alive within her family. Warren Morris (dec.), Jacob's uncle and mentor, handed down the responsibility of language to him and his cousin Joel Deaves. Jacob also teaches language and dance at Nowra East Public School through his own business, Ngundahmurra.

Lorna Munro, or 'Yilinhi', is a Wiradjuri and Gamilaroi woman, multidisciplinary artist and regular radio and podcast host at Sydney's Radio Skid Row. A long-time active member of her Redfern/Waterloo community, her work is informed by her passion and well-studied insight in areas such as culture, history, politics and popular culture. Lorna has travelled the world showcasing her skills and distinctive style of poetry and political commentary. She was also the sole designer and creator of Sydney's–and possibly Australia's–first initiative to teach Aboriginal language through poetry, in partnership with Red Room Poetry in 2015. Throughout her career she has been on stage, in films and on paper. She compiled and edited *Paper Dreaming: Our Stories Our Way* for Cambridge University Press (2015). Lorna continues to work tirelessly mastering many art forms, raising funds, and supporting and advocating for her community and her people on the local, national and international stage. In 2019 Lorna was announced as a recipient of the Wheeler Centre's Next Chapter Fellowship.

Maureen Jipyiliya Nampijinpa O'Keefe is an artist, writer, storyteller and storykeeper. Her family comes from the Devil's Marbles area, also known as Karlu Karlu, and she is a Kaytetye-Warlpiri woman born and raised in Ali-Curung, south-east of Tennant Creek.

Bruce Pascoe published and edited *Australian Short Stories* magazine from 1982 to 1999, has won the Prime Minister's Literary Award for Young Adult fiction (*Fog a Dox*) in 2013, the Australian Literature Award 1999, Radio National Short Story 1998 and FAW Short Story 2010. His books include *Night Animals*, *Shark*, *Ocean*, *Bloke* (Penguin, 2009), *Cape Otway*, *Chainsaw File* (Oxford, 2010), *Convincing Ground*, *Fog a Dox* (Magabala, 2012), *Little Red Yellow and Black Book, Mrs Whitlam* (Magabala, 2016) and *Seahorse* (Magabala, 2015). He is of Yuin, Bunurong/Tasmanian heritage and lives in East Gippsland, and is a board member of Aboriginal Corporation for Languages. *Dark Emu*, a history of Aboriginal agriculture, was published by Magabala in 2014 and won the New South Wales Premier's Book of the Year Award in 2016 and was performed by Bangarra Dance Theatre in 2018. He was awarded the Lifetime Achievement in Literature Award by the Australia Council in 2018.

Nick Paton is a proud descendant of the Ngunawal people. Having spent a number of years working on music education programs at the NSW Department of Education, Nick is passionate about poetry, writing and the limitless possibilities of engaging with Elders and traditional language custodians in order to study many of the estimated 600 First Nations language dialects of Australia. Nick is a journalist with the *Koori Mail* newspaper and resides on the lands of the Bundjalung Nation. Nick is studying a Bachelor of Indigenous Knowledge at Southern Cross University with major subjects and interests focused around traditional Indigenous land management practices and knowledge systems.

Ryan Prehn is a Worimi poet and, proudly, no two of his bios are the same. He doesn't want to list the accolades and accomplishments stuff, because that doesn't mean anything to him. What matters is connection and story. Come talk to him to find out more.

Celestine Rowe originates from Papunya NT … from a long line of musicians n artists. Celestine is a writer who has travelled around australia performing spoken word since she was 16 years old. She joined desert divas in 2013 n 2014 where her poetry was transformed to songs … she is returning to Bush bands bash with her political … uplifting and inspiring words.

Brenda Saunders is a Wiradjuri writer and artist living in Sydney. She is an active member of FNAWN (First Nations

Aboriginal Writers Network) and is a mentor for Black Cockatoo, the Emerging Indigenous Poets site at Verity La. Brenda has written three poetry books and her recent collection, 'Inland Sea', is ready for a publisher. Her poems and reviews appear in anthologies and journals, including *Australian Poetry Journal*, *Overland*, *Southerly*, *Westerly* and *Plumwood Mountain*. She has won several awards including the 2014 Scanlon Book Prize (Australian Poetry), the 2018 Oodgeroo Noonuccal Prize (Queensland Poetry) and the Joanne Burns Award for Prose Poetry (Spineless Wonders).

Proud Gunai Woman **Kirli Saunders** is an award-winning international children's author, poet, teacher and emerging artist. She leads Poetry in First Languages, delivered by Red Room Poetry. Kirli's debut picture book, *The Incredible Freedom Machines*, was shortlisted for the Prime Minister's Literary Awards and CBCA notables. Her poetry collection, *Kindred*, was highly commended in black&write! She is the inaugural winner of the WA Premier's Daisy Utemorrah Award and University of Canberra Aboriginal and Torres Strait Islander Poetry Prize. Kirli is 2020 NSW Aboriginal Woman of the Year. She was guest writer for the Australian Embassy in Jakarta and Bali (2019).

Nicole Smede is a vocalist, musician and emerging poet. Her work explores a reclamation and reconnection with ancestry and country through poetry and song. Born, living and creating on Dharawal Country, Nicole's ancestors are Worimi, English, Irish and German. www.nicolesmede.com

Stiff Gins is one of Australia's best known and most loved Indigenous acts. Featuring Nardi Simpson and Kaleena Briggs, Stiff Gins combines stunning harmonies and wicked humour to transport you to a world of joy, spirit and song. Eleven years ago, their moniker was reclamation of an offensive reference to Aboriginal women, a banner to guide their music in the direction of strength and pride. Three albums and countless shows later, the name has become synonymous with musical excellence. They have travelled the world, received prestigious awards and created a loyal fan base with their heartfelt songs and emotive performances. They've performed in the Middle East and remote communities across Australia and developed a musical friendship that has transformed them both.

Lyndsay Urqhuart is a Koori Munkata Yuin woman growing up in the Dharawal community of western Sydney. Passionate about remembering and sharing her cultures with her family and as a teacher of Indigenous arts, Lyndsay is a public education guide. As a practising Indigenous oral historian, Lyndsay works as a documentary filmmaker as a way of preserving and sharing important information and perspectives. Lyndsay works as a curator and as a multidisciplinary artist in the area of communications, so as to share and help educate communities about the world's oldest continuing cultures. These are the first poems Lyndsay has written since primary school.

Born in Meanjin in 1990, **Ellen van Neerven** is an award-winning writer and editor of Mununjali Yugambeh and Dutch heritage with strong ancestral ties to south-east Queensland. They write fiction, poetry, plays and non-fiction.

Samuel Wagan Watson is a Brisbane-based writer of Germanic and Wunjaburra ancestry. His body of work was granted the Patrick White Literary Award in 2018. Collections of his poetry have won accolades and been successfully translated overseas. A late exploration of his short story writing has found a place in journals such as *Cordite*, the *Saturday Paper* and the *Chicago Quarterly Review*, and in the anthology *Caring for Country*. He is published by University of Queensland Press.

Adrian Webster, known as Ado, is a proud Yuin and Thunghutti murrin (person). He was born in Naora (Nowra) next to Bungalii (the Shoalhaven River) and has spent his life growing up on the south coast of New South Wales, and will always be there learning stories, songs and dances that connect him strongly to the ocean as a katungal murrin (saltwater person) and the land as he continues to uphold his responsibilities to love, respect and look after the land and all life that inhabits it.

Kaitlen Wellington is a descendant from the Jerrinja people, Yuin Nation, who is studying a Bachelor of Arts at University of Wollongong. She is a young emerging writer who finds inspiration in the land and contemporary expressions of culture. Kaitlen believes in the power of storytelling and intends to explore varying forms during her unfolding career.

Melanie Mununggurr Williams is a Djapu mother, writer, poet and spoken word artist. She writes in both English and Dhuwal (Yolngu Matha dialect) about identity, family, current social issues. Melanie also uses her writing as a platform for raising awareness about autism. She often weaves Dhuwal throughout her writing as a way of decolonising literature and the arts. In 2019 Melanie travelled to 6 countries and performed at many festivals around Australia. Her first book of poetry for young adults will be released by Penguin Random House in the near future.

PERMISSIONS

'A Dog Barking', *Wild Bees,* Martin Harrison, kindly reproduced with permission from UWA Publishing.

The lyrics of the song 'Longing, Wanting' by Stiff Gins has been republished with their permission. 'Longing, Wanting' is among a collection of songs commissioned by the Australian Museum for its project 'The Spirit of Things–Sound of Objects', which explores the living stories and songs within Aboriginal cultural material.

'Disconnection' by Kirli Saunders was originally published in *Kindred* (Magabala, 2019)

Editor: Jeanine Leane
Red Room Poetry, Artistic Director: Tamryn Bennett
Red Room Poetry, Director External Relations:
Sally Marwood
Red Room Poetry, Manager First Nations Programs:
Kirli Saunders
Red Room Poetry, Senior Project Manager:
Anne-Marie Te Whiu
Magabala, Publisher: Rachel Bin Salleh
Cover Artist: Kamsani Bin Salleh

Red Room Poetry is a not-for-profit organisation whose vision is to make poetry in meaningful ways. Our poetic projects are created in collaboration with a spectrum of poets, communities and partners for positive impact in core areas of environment, amplification, First Nations, youth and marginalised voices. We aim to make poetry highly visible, vibrant, relevant and accessible, especially to those who face the greatest barriers to creative opportunities. Care, quality, imagination, invention, integrity and collaboration underpin our work. Red Room Poetry advocates for professional payment of poets ensuring sustainability, quality creation and the future of Australian literature.

redroomcompany.org

Red Room Poetry acknowledges all our partners and supporters: Oranges and Sardines Foundation and the many generous individuals and supporters across the history of our First Nations projects who have enabled the commissioning and creation of this poetry.

Australian Government | Australia Council for the Arts

NSW GOVERNMENT

COPYRIGHTAGENCY CULTURAL FUND

NELSON MEERS FOUNDATION

United Nations Educational, Scientific and Cultural Organization | Australian National Commission for UNESCO

BUNDANON TRUST

MIROMAA ABORIGINAL LANGUAGE & TECHNOLOGY CENTRE

RECONCILIATION AUSTRALIA